Mies van der Rohe Award for European Architecture

Mies van der Rohe Award for European Architecture

Butterworth Architecture
London Boston Singapore
Sydney Toronto Wellington

 PART OF REED INTERNATIONAL P.L.C.

First published 1990.
© Butterworth & Co. (Publishers) Ltd, 1990.
© V+K Publishing, 1990.

British Library Cataloguing in Publication Data

Applied for

ISBN 0 408 50084 0

Library of Congress Cataloguing in Publication Data

Applied for

ISBN 0 408 50084 0

Cover illustrations: Borges & Irmão Bank, Alvaro Siza.

Contents

Rules for the Mies van der Rohe Award for European Architecture

The European space is composed of an emulsion of natural and cultural, vernacular and canonical, and traditional and artificial elements. Modern architecture must assume this ambiguity, project it towards the future and offset the natural wear to which forms are subject by means of a symmetrical process of innovation; a process that has been presided over by works that introduced into an architectural tradition a new inflection or added value that can only be qualified as *artistic*.

The purpose of the Award is to detect and highlight such works – of which the Mies van der Rohe Pavilion of Barcelona is a genuine symbol – whose innovational character acts as an orientation or even a *manifesto*. This is why the Award Jury shall represent the institutions involved, but while reflecting the feeling and cultural intention that endows the Award with both a symbolic and pedagogic value. In this way, expression is given to the concern of the E.E.C. Commission for the survival of the European city which – often walled in between the impersonal and the domestic, between the official and the suburban – must recover its own tradition from certain uncommon but exemplary works. With this purpose in mind, the Commission institutes a single biennial award, whose organization is entrusted to the Mies van der Rohe Foundation of Barcelona on the basis of these Rules.

1. The Commission of the European Communities creates the 'Mies van der Rohe Pavilion, Barcelona' International Architecture Award. This Award shall be granted to the author or authors of an architectural work constructed in the area of the E.E.C. countries within a space of two years immediately prior to the granting of the Award (this period may be extended at the discretion of the Jury for the first holding of the Award Contest), whose formal value aims at a renewal of the architectural property of the European city.

2. The Award Contest is open to all the authors of works that have been completed within the two years prior to the granting of the Award, without the need for prior submission or guarantee of any type.

3. The Award shall be granted on a biennial basis as of 1987 by the E.E.C. Commission, at the proposal of a Jury composed of acknowledged experts in the field of architecture and of architectural criticism, appointed in this way: two members by the E.E.C. Cultural Commissioner, one of whom shall hold the position of President of the Jury; two members by the European

Parliament; two members by the Mies van der Rohe Foundation of Barcelona, one of whom shall carry out the functions of Secretary of the Jury; and one member by the Council of Europe. These appointments shall be valid for two successive holdings of the Award Contest and they may not be extended or renewed beyond this limit.

4. For the purposes of the selection of candidates, a Committee of Experts composed of an ample number of Members shall be formed, and each Expert shall propose a maximum of three candidates for submission to the consideration of the Jury.

The circumstance of belonging to the Committee of Experts shall not exclude the submission of works carried out by the Committee Members.

The appointment of the Committee of Experts shall be made by the E.E.C. Cultural Commissioner at the proposal of the Secretary of the Mies van der Rohe Award Contest.

The final list of selected candidates shall be drawn up at the proposal of the Committee of Experts and be supplemented with the Candidates that were to be freely selected by the Members of the Jury.

5. Following the pertinent analysis of information and the subsequent debate, the Jury shall grant the Award by secret ballot and absolute majority of its Members.

6. The holding of the Award Contest, and the pertinent meetings and deliberations, as well as the expenses derived from the required communications, shall be for the account, on a coordinated basis, of the institutions represented on the Jury.

7. The act of voting for the designation of the Winner shall be performed secretly, and the Jury shall make its decision known forthwith in the course of a celebration organized for such purpose at the Headquarters of the Mies van der Rohe Pavilion.

8. The presentation of the Award, which shall be a sculptural piece evoking the Mies van der Rohe Pavilion of Barcelona, shall be made by the E.E.C. Cultural Commissioner in a solemn, protocolary ceremony.

9. The Award may not be declared vacant. There shall be a single, indivisible Award for each holding. Acceptance of the Award entails the prior acceptance of these Rules, of the composition of the Jury and of the Jury's decision.

Act of the Jury of the Mies van der Rohe Award for European Architecture

On September 24, 1988, at 4.30 p.m., the Jury of the European Architecture Award 'Mies van der Rohe', promoted by the E.E.C. Cultural Commission, the European Parliament, the Council of Europe and the Barcelona City Council through the Mies van der Rohe Foundation, met at the Palau de la Virreina in Barcelona.

The Jury, presided over by the British architect **Kenneth Frampton**, is composed of the architects **Hans Hollein** (Vienna), **Vittorio Gregotti** (Milan), **François Burckhardt** (Paris), **Ricardo Bofill** (Barcelona) and **Ignasi de Solà-Morales** (Barcelona), who acts as Secretary. The architect **Alessandro Giulianelli** also attends the meeting as the personal representative of the E.E.C. Cultural Commissioner, with no intervening powers.

The Jury originally considered a selection of some 70 buildings made by the members of the Jury themselves at their previous meeting in Brussels and those presented by a Committee of Experts of the different countries of the E.E.C.

The final selection of the Award, in accordance with the rules and guidelines established by the Jury itself, will be selected from buildings finished during the last four years in an E.E.C. country by a European architect.

The Jury first thought of making a restricted selection of five candidates from which the Award would be chosen, but revised this proposal during the meeting. After an extensive debate, all the members agreed to make a wider selection more representative of the real diversity of trends of the best European architecture. Since variety itself is characteristic of the European specificity, the Jury felt that such variety, reflected in a diversity of works, would best exemplify the criteria of innovation, urban sense, and historic consciousness of tradition.

The proclamation of the winner of the first European Architecture Award 'Mies van der Rohe', will take place in Barcelona on December 8, 1988, at the Mies van der Rohe Barcelona Pavilion, with the assistance of the E.E.C. Cultural Commissioner, the Mayor of Barcelona, and other European authorities of the Institutions promoting the Award.

The Award will consist of a singular object referring to the Award and an amount in cash equal to 50.000 Ecus.

After a second debate, the Jury proceeded to the election of the awarded

building and architect. After a succession of votes the Jury agreed to grant the European Architecture Award, 'Mies van der Rohe' to the Borges & Irmão Bank in Vila do Conde (Portugal), constructed between 1982 and 1986 and to the architect **Alvaro Siza Viera**, designer of the building.
The Jury passed a resolution not to make this decision public until the E.E.C. Cultural Commissioner deems it appropriate.

Barcelona, October, 1988

The Mies van der Rohe Award for European Architectural: Notes on the Inaugural Prize

For five hundred years our locus of the modern has been gravitating towards the West and, above all for the last century or so, towards an almost mythical New World. Now, quite suddenly, in a manner that uncannily corresponds to the approaching millennium, our idea of the modern is suffering a change and nothing seems now to be new, in the sense that it once was. In large measure, this is due to a constantly accelerating rate of change that increasingly renders every innovation obsolete before it has had a chance to become assimilated. This rapid techno-economic transformation has disconcerting implications at many levels, not least of which is the fact that the natural environment is beginning to break down under the impact of such rapacious development. This crisis has implications for architecture at many different levels and in part this prize is oriented towards compensating, at a critical level, for the ecological and cultural disruptions caused by recent urban expansion and development. With the current upheavals in Eastern Europe, the emergence of the European Community as an independent political force and the promise of some form of continental federation by 1992, the star of the Old World is rising in both an economic and a cultural sense. While the Mies van der Rohe Award for European Architecture must be situated in just such a context, it has also to be seen as a response to the decade-old, American International Pritzker Prize for Architecture. At the same time the Award is not simply the fruit of transatlantic competitiveness, for the two honours address very different constituencies. Where the Pritzker is categorically international in scope, the Mies van der Rohe Award for European Architecture seeks solely to encourage architectural excellence in Europe and with this to further the cultural identity and strength of the region. In the words of the inaugural conditions, the aim is to express *'the concern of the E.E.C. Commission for the survival of the European city which, often walled-in between the impersonal and the domestic, between the official and suburban, must recover its own tradition from certain uncommon but exemplary works'*.

With this in mind the first Award Jury convened in June 1988 in order to select a single prize-winner out of some 24 nominees. This limited number of candidates had been selected by 17 appointed experts, representing between them the member states of the E.E.C., with some of the larger nations being represented by more than one expert. While the jury could also nominate candidates for the prize, it was nonetheless restricted to advancing the name of a single European architect or design group as meriting the Award for a building erected in the E.E.C. over the past two years. Since this was the inaugural occasion, this time-limit was somewhat extended, at the Jury's discretion, in order to admit slightly older works that were judged as having made a significant contribution to the European scene. Our decision to award the inaugural prize to **Alvaro Siza**, for his Borges & Irmão Bank completed in Vila do Conde in 1986, should not be construed as any kind of negative judgement on the other works. As one might imagine, many criteria affected our final selection and obviously it would have been easier if we had been in a position to present more than one Award. Although we had to arrive at a consensus about a single work, it is necessary to acknowledge that among the short list there were many excellent examples of the different contemporary genres that go to characterise our *post-modern* era, ranging from so-called *high-tech* works to buildings that evoke traditional forms. In our first cut we tried to select the best representatives of the different genres, thereby attempting to transcend, as far as is possible, the more superficial aspects of style. While it is by now a fairly futile exercise to classify all these various genres by name, I will nonetheless use this introduction to comment on the more general issues raised by certain buildings that were given particular consideration by the Jury. What follows is therefore an unavoidably subjective critique of some of the works pre-selected and nominated and, inevitably, this all too cursory assessment is expressly my own. Other members of the Jury would surely stress other exemplars and thus raise in consequence a quite different set of issues. While recognising the risks entailed in positing any kind of taxonomy, it is nonetheless remarkable how most of the nominated works fall into one or other of what, by now, are commonly accepted genres. Thus, the overall spectrum nominated may be categorised, in retrospect, as coming under such headings as High-Tech, Neo-Rationalist, Contextualist, Minimalist, Structuralist, and even Neo-Historicist. Some of these categories display more clearly identifiable characteristics than others and moreover, as always, subtle distinctions may invariably be found within the same category. Thus while the works of the High-Tech architects – **Richard Rogers, Norman Foster and Renzo Piano** – all display to varying degrees the same concern for the transparent expression of structure and for a form of detailing that reflects the mode of production, the specific expression of the service component in relation to the structure varies in each instance. So while they embrace the same techno-ethical code, it may be argued that where **Rogers** is flamboyantly expressive at the level of services, **Foster** is the more consequent with regard to structure, and **Piano** the architect who gives the most attention to the inflections imposed by the given mode of production.

The works of the Neo-Rationalists, on the other hand, are to be distinguished by their strict adherence to the normative order of plan typology, irrespective of whether the approach is more technocratic, as in the case of **Josef Paul Kleihues'** Neukoln Hospital built near Berlin in 1986, or more metaphysical, as in the case of the works submitted on behalf of **Oswald Mathias Ungers**. With regard to the latter I have in mind the complex that Ungers designed for the Frankfurt Trade Fair or, say, such works as the Karlsruhe Regional Library or the Polar Institute in Bremen. We see that even within this highly disciplined approach wide variations are to be found. Thus, while **Mario Botta** remains anchored within the Neo-Rationalist camp, in other instances the classical citations seem too direct and one remains uncertain in such cases as to whether the buildings in question should be classified as Neo-Rationalist or Neo-Historicist. The works of **Aldo Rossi** are extremely ambiguous in this regard and one is aware of a number of other architects who were formally of a Late Modern persuasion and who now display a similar ambiguity. In many instances the nominations were strongly influenced by *contextual* considerations, as in the case of **Gino Valle's** Giudecca Housing in Venice of 1986 or **Colquhoun** and **Miller's** Whitechapel Art Gallery of 1985.

What is decisive in all this is not so much the overt style as the organisation in depth. This is most evident, say, in **Gerd Feseld** and **Peter Bayerer's** building for Berlin, where the superficial *high-tech* surface seems to be denied by the extremely rational, not to say classical, organisation of the plan. Such deceptive appearances serve to remind us that within the Western tradition, Neo-Rationalism is largely a derivative of the Neo-Classical line.

The boundary separating Neo-Rationalism from Neo-Historicism is at times so thin as to enable one to pass almost imperceptibly from one ideological fix to the next. **Riviere**, **Ortega** and **Capitel's** reformulation of Madrid's Puerta del Sol (1986) clearly lies on this frontier, as does **Rossi's** Capelli Ardente of 1987. **Colquhoun** and **Miller's** pedimented terrace housing also clearly crosses this line, as does **James Stirling's** somewhat willful, not to say gratuitous, attitude towards both traditional types and tectonic details. This much is evident in his Wissenschaftszentrum completed in the Tiergarten, Berlin in 1987, despite the rigour of its detailing. Similarly, for all their previous commitment to the modern tradition, the small bank built on Rhodes to the designs of the **Antonakakis** partnership in 1985 suffers from similar ambiguities, and much the same may be claimed, in a different context, for the corner infill block built in Antwerp in 1988 to the designs of the Belgian architectural design team **A.W.G.** While not as outrageously collagiste as, say, **Stirling's** recent work, these late modern pieces seem nonetheless to gravitate towards a kind of decorative deliquescence.

Save for the exfoliating, electronically controlled sun screens of the Institut du Monde Arabe, there is nothing decorative about the Neo-Minimalism practised by **Jean Nouvel**. However, **Nouvel** seems to be too technologically indulgent to qualify as a rigorous Minimalist. His particular form of playful, indeed often brilliant, rhetoric favours an uncommon combination of extravagant structural gestures with modest and highly expedient, *off-the peg,* mass-produced components.

Elsewhere a kind of Constructivist-Minimalism has been advanced in different ways by the Austrian **Gustav Peichl** and by the young Dutch architect **Rem Koolhaas**. Peichl's late Constructivism seems influenced to an almost equal degree by **Hans Poelzig's** expressionism and **Otto Wagner's** tectonic precision, see his Phosphate Elimination Plant in Berlin. **Koolhaas** aspires to an altogether *cooler,* one might say dispensable, approach to modern form, as is evident from his Dance Theatre completed in The Hague in 1987, which to put it bluntly is crudely detailed. Where **Koolhaas** continues to emphasise a highly abstract Neo-Suprematist attitude towards form, one that is more graphic than structural, **Peichl** remains committed to the expressive potential of technology down to the last bolt.

The Plaça dels Països Catalans built outside the Sants station in Barcelona to
the designs of **Helio Piñón** and **Albert Viaplana** in 1983 is surely one of the
most sublime works to date in the Minimalist vein. The light techno-topo-
graphic manner demonstrated in this singular urban piece puts these architects into a class of their own, although at times they display a curious af-
finity for the laconic structural form of the Porto School.

Structuralism may be defined as an approach that stresses the detailed
articulation of space and its full integration into the tectonic of a given
work. Despite its familiarity it remains a quintessentially Dutch form, represented on this occasion by the works of **Theo Bosch** and **Herman Hertzberger**,
that is by **Bosch's** Faculty of Arts for Amsterdam University of 1984 and by
Hertzberger's IBA housing in Berlin and his so-called Apollo Schools in Amsterdam. While **Bosch's** piece is an appropriate form of urban infill, reinforc-
ing the existing street pattern by its scale and by the *meta-street* incorporated within, **Hertzberger** remains one of the most didactic and critical architects practising today, and his buildings invariably attain a fusion of formal
brilliance and socio-anthropological relevance that is hard to match. As
Hertzberger puts it, *'I try to make my architecture appropriate in order that
it may be appropriated.'* The stepped central theatrical spaces of his recent
schools are typical in this regard in that, by serving the school community in
different ways, they afford different kinds of experience. In the first place
they may be appropriated for the purposes of assembly or theatrical per-
formance; in the second, however, they become informal *spaces of public
appearance,* where children may casually meet, talk, sit or do their home-
work. Typologically speaking, these spaces may be said to approximate the
stepped esplanades of some miniature antique city. One cannot leave
Hertzberger without remarking on the way in which his contextual response
is never quietistic or oversimplified, as is evident from his infill housing for
Amsterdam, where the scale and the stoop-form of the existing fabric finds
itself reinterpreted in a dynamic and unsentimental way.

Moderate-income urban housing remains now as ever a European penchant,
and among some of the finest nominations submitted for the prize were
works of this genre. Mention must be made in this regard of a number of
successful recent examples, including **Siza's** remarkable reinterpretation of

the modern Dutch housing tradition in the Schilderswijk, The Hague, which is so exceptionally sensitive at the level of both material and type, and the more abstract, more mega-urban pieces nominated independently from the studios of **Henri Ciriani**, **Henri Gaudin** and **Wilhelm Holzbauer**.

When all is said and done, the creative vortex of the European renewal of late modern architecture seems still to be grounded in the Iberian peninsula, from which works of exceptional quality continue to emanate, from Sevilla, Barcelona, Madrid and Oporto and from many other Spanish and Portuguese provinces. In this regard much attention was paid by the Jury to **Rafael Moneo's** quite brilliant Roman archeological museum completed in Mérida in 1986, not only for the strength of its tectonic form but also for its urban responsiveness and for its subtle approach to history of the place, at so many different levels. By audaciously recognising that not all archaic ruins are equally sacrosanct and that, in any event, they have to be enlivened and integrated into our modern way of life, **Moneo** was able to implant his museum over the excavations of the original Roman city, thereby establishing a dialogue, as it were, between living cross-walls and dead foundations. In so doing he enabled the visitor to walk quite literally between two realities, thereby causing them to experience, as in a catacomb, something of the urban presence of a lost Roman past. It is surely a stroke of genius that by the judicious introduction of a tunnel one may now pass from this nether world to the twin Roman amphitheatres situated at the nearby site. With its concrete cross-walls faced in Roman brick, history also appears in this work at a more metaphorical level, engendering a number of typological and constructional associations wherein one may pass, let us say, from medieval warehouse to modern factory without ever being able to settle on one architectonic reference rather than another.

Mention must also be made of the brilliant young Spanish engineer-architect **Santiago Calatrava**, whose works, one imagines, will continue to be nominated for this prize since the energy, lucidity and brilliance of his achievement is already beyond dispute. On this occasion his art was predictably represented by the remarkable Bach de Roda / Felip II bridge completed in the inner suburbs of Barcelona in 1987. Like **Moneo's** Mérida Museum, **Calatrava's** bridge is an object lesson in maximizing the urban potential of a one-off structure. Once again we have a work that functions at a number of levels at once, serving in this instance as an *urban fix* in terms of the road and rail approaches to the no-man's-land of the Barcelona outskirts. At the same time it functions as a circulatory matrix for linking public parks on either side of the rail line. One should perhaps mention in passing the perennial Iberian prowess in the field of landscape design and cite among the finer nominated examples of this skill **Martorell, Bohigas and Mackay's** Creueta del Coll Park, realised in Barcelona in 1987.

In granting the inaugural prize to **Siza**, the European Community effectively honours not only an exceptional work by a very distinguished architect but also the *regional* culture of which he is the most prominent representative. I am alluding to the so-called School of Oporto, from which we received other nominations besides those representing the work of the **Siza** Studio. Among these other submissions one recalls a municipal building designed by **Siza's** lesser known but equally talented peer, **Alcino Soutinho**, and a house from the hand of his prime pupil, **Eduardo Souto de Moura**, together with a stadium under construction in Braga to the designs of **Goncalo Sousa Byrne**. When one looks back over this whole event nothing is perhaps more surprising than the exceptional gap separating the oldest from the youngest of the architects pre-selected and nominated. Thus while we were presented with numerous works designed by architects in their mid-forties, the oldest architect pre-selected was **Ignazio Gardella**, who at 84, after over half a century of practise, is still decidedly active. There is perhaps nothing more moving in this anthology of the Award than the funerary monument by **Gardella**, realised in Brescia in 1985, for this impressive exercise in precision brickwork has the kind of maturity and vigour that one generally expects from someone much younger. It is surely a good omen for the future of European culture when an almost mythical veteran can still be seen as participating as intensely in the present as he has in the past.

Kenneth Frampton

Borges & Irmão Bank | Alvaro Siza

Awarded Project: Borges & Irmão Bank | Vila do Conde, Portugal | 1982-1986

Alvaro Siza

The Borges & Irmão Bank, designed by **Alvaro Siza**, is located in the historic centre of Vila do Conde, which is dominated by monumental buildings of granite and stucco, such as the main Church and the Saint Clara Monastery. The bank is situated on an elongated site in Rua 25 de Abril. An urban master plan, which preceded **Siza's** project, had radically changed the area, and envisaged a piazza between the gardens of the houses to be entered via a new street. For this reason the site of the project occupies the corner of two streets. The demolition of the existing house presented **Siza** with a site devoid of building content.

In his Borges & Irmão Bank one can read all the spatial ideas which had been experimented with while the form was being developed. Until the very last moment, **Siza** left open the possibility of modification. The bank presents itself as an exception to the fabric of the other buildings in the street. It is precisely the use of this language, intentionally contrasting with the immediate surroundings, which allows **Siza's** architecture to establish long-distance relationships with the monuments of the city. The building, with its prismatic purism and white colour, contrasts with the context, while its volume and importance are more in line with the existing buildings along the street. A direct reference to the architecture of these buildings would seem forced. The building is thus established as a kind of crossing of scales, in a relationship simultaneously of dialogue with and distance from the monuments and the urban fabric from which they arise. This relationship adjusts the character of the building to its cultural location in the town.

The bank of Vila do Conde belongs to a series of projects for bank buildings. It provides a sort of anthology of formal and methodological references to **Siza's** earlier work. In this design **Siza** has tended to *purify his formal vocabulary, using elementary volumes and smooth surfaces.* The complexity of the building is achieved through an unusual accumulation of different spatial and figurative themes. The result is an exceptional density of spatial events, with a strong visual impact. In spite of the small scale, it rivals the major civic and religious monuments of the city.

The building consists of a main block surrounded by an architecture of ramps, stairs and access routes. Two corners are curved, which produces the impression not of four, but of two continuous facades. These are very differ-

1933 Born in Matosinhos, Portugal.
1949-1955 Studied at the School of Architecture, University of Oporto, Portugal.
1954 Started an architectural office in Oporto, Portugal.
1955-1958 Worked with Fernando Tavora.
1958 Started an architectural office with Fernando Tavora.
1965 Professor, School of Architecture, University of Oporto, Portugal.
1982 Awarded the Architecture Prize by the Portuguese Department of the International Association of Art Critics.
1987 Portuguese Architects Association Award.
1988 Awarded the Gold Medal of the Spanish Architectural Association.
1988 Alvar Aalto Medal, Finland.
1988 Awarded the Prince of Wales Prize in Urban Design by Harvard University, Cambridge, U.S.A.
1988 Mies van der Rohe Award for European Architecture, Barcelona, Spain.

Visiting Professor at the Federal Polytechnic Lausanne, Switzerland and the University of Pennsylvania, U.S.A.

Major works
1977-1979 Co-operative housing, Bairro de Malagueira, Evora, Portugal.
1981-1985 House of Avalino Duarte, Ovar, Portugal.
1982-1986 Borges & Irmão Bank, Vila do Conde, Portugal.
1988 Two dwellings with shops, The Hague, The Netherlands

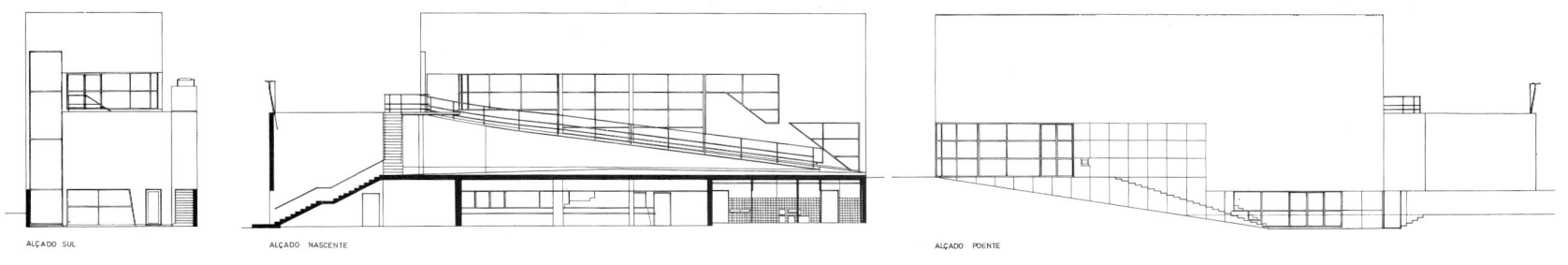

ALÇADO SUL   ALÇADO NASCENTE   ALÇADO POENTE

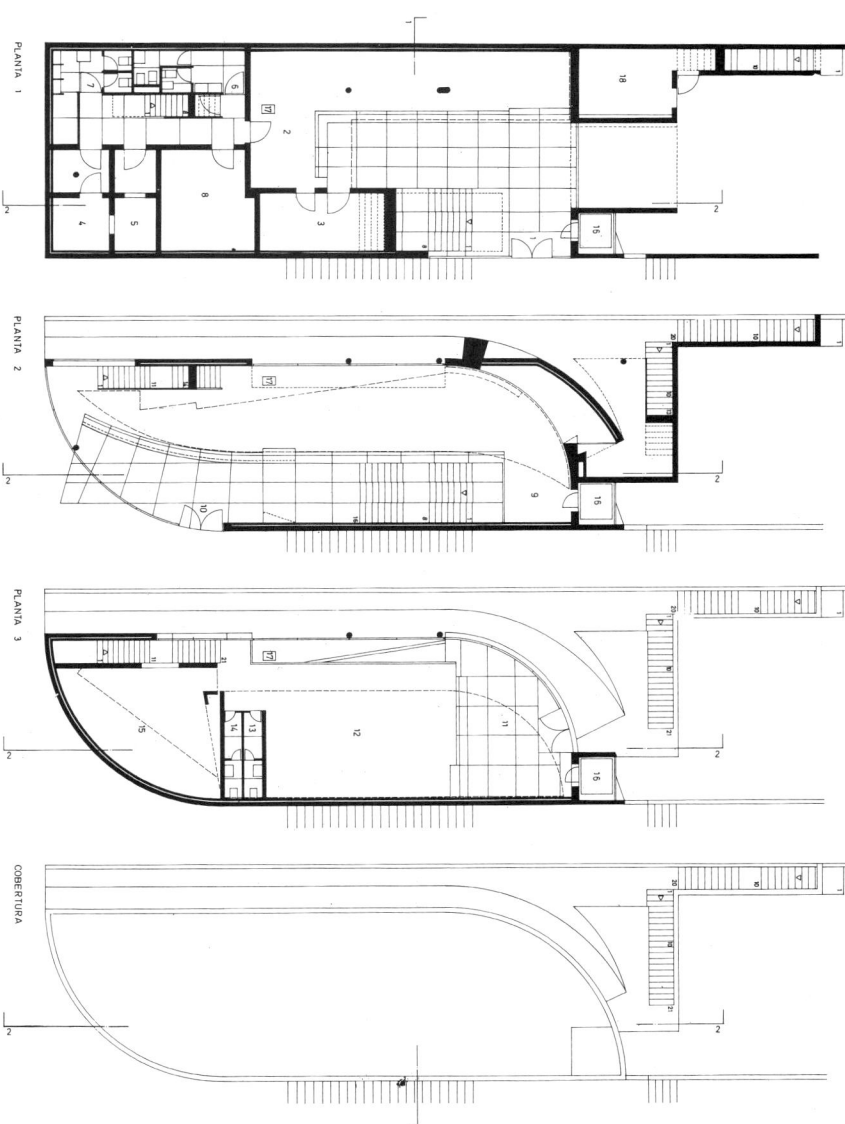

PLANTA 1

PLANTA 2

PLANTA 3

COBERTURA

ent from one another. The north-west facade is entirely smooth, with the windows and the marble-cladding flush to the white plaster. The south-east facade is enlivened by a ramp, a staircase, a large glazed wall, which is pulled back, a fully glazed corner at the upper level and a full-height, transparent lift. The transparency of the glazed wall makes it possible to read clearly the system of internal circulation. In the exterior of the building there is a continuity of marble-cladding: on the wall, on the steps and on the sides of the external public staircases. The marble of the public atrium floor, inside the building, extends to the outside.

The building has four levels: the lower ground floor, which is also the garden level, the ground floor, the first floor and the roof level. Each floor has its own public entrance. At the lower level entrance is from the street, at the ground floor from the corner of the two streets, and at the upper level both from the ramp from the street and from the stairs from the garden. The interior space is determined by a series of distorting effects, which oppose the static qualities of an orthogonal plan. These include the curvature of the corners, the flow of the public along the counter which ends against a staircase, the asymmetry of the glazed surfaces, the divergent movements of the ceilings and the different claddings.

Borges & Irmăo Bank | Alvaro Siza

The Delicate Architecture of Alvaro Siza

In **Meyer Schapiro's** famous article *'On the Aesthetic Attitude in Romanesque Art'* (1947), he refers to the epitaph which the master architect **Gilberto** chose for his cathedral in Toulouse: *Gilbertus, vir non incertus.* The ambiguity of this medieval Latin epithet was clearly intentional: the artist is not only *not unknown,* renowned even, but also *certain of his skills,* master of his trade.

'If my works are not finished, if they are interfered with or modified,' **Alvaro Siza** wrote in 1980, *'this has nothing whatever to do with any aesthetic principle nor with a belief in open ended creations. It has more to do with the frustrating impossibility of ever completing them and with the obstacles I am incapable of avoiding.'*

The disparity between these two approaches to architectural creation is reflected in our aesthetic appreciation of classical, and (according to **Schapiro**) medieval culture on the one hand, and modern culture on the other. In the former, Western man encounters conformity — adaptation to nature, to the city, to tradition; adherence to rules, methods and metier.

Such conformity is entirely absent in the work of **Alvaro Siza**, who was recently awarded Europe's highest architectural prize. For the masters of the Modern Movement, instilled with the scientific illusion they inherited from the nineteenth century, contemporary architecture can and must be self-generating. Based on the new realities of technology, the functional programme, economy of construction and rationality of form, it seems to return to Platonism and ancient aesthetics. These maintained that each work represented a unique synthesis of the rational order of things, its consistency being its logic.

Alvaro Siza sees things in a very different way. *'Any design is an earnest endeavour to capture the nuances of a given instant in a transient reality.'* No consistency is more valid than that which concedes aesthetic value to a work of art or architecture. There is no global, absolute, or perfect architecture. *'From the shelter of isolated fragments we seek the space that surrounds man,'* **Siza** adds.

Siza's career is hardly the kind one would expect of someone who chooses a paradigmatic work as the subject of a European architectural prize: his oeuvre is not very prolific; alongside the many commissions that were never realized, it includes small buildings on the outskirts of Oporto and a number of half-completed, larger ensembles. His work presents few re-usable models, for there are no *'ready new solutions for the new conditions of modern life'*. It is not for him to produce works that will serve as models for other locations and other cities.

Whilst demanding that his architecture should also reflect *transitory qualities,* **Alvaro Siza's** architecture is exciting for its candour and the lucidity with which it demonstrates the difficult, and ultimately irresolvable, conflict of the artist versus the user, innovation versus tradition, natural environment versus urban artifice.

What is fascinating about the Award-winning building, the Borges & Irmão Bank in the small town of Vila do Conde, is the deliberate vulnerability on which the decisions of the project are based. This weakness has generated a work of art that avoids triviality, demagoguery and imitation; above all it is endowed with a strength that is both essential and provisional.

Those who seek integration of the architecture in its surroundings will be disappointed: the smooth white stucco surface and brilliant marbles of the facades of the little bank building seem to oppose the shape and texture of the modest, surrounding, 19th-century houses. But it would be wrong to infer from this that **Alvaro Siza** is insensitive to the building's urban location. Its alignment with Rua 25 de Abril (an important date in recent Portuguese history) and with a newly created street attest to **Siza's** civic sensibility and explain the generous corner at their curved intersection that gives the building its characteristic form. Also the volume, single yet multiple through the combination of different dimensions, approaches the scale of the surrounding buildings dialectically opposed to the bank building scheme.

In **Siza's** architecture there is not just a single geometry, but many. The organization of his buildings clearly reflects the effort undertaken to devise a system to accommodate the parts. In plan and section the buildings of **Alvaro Siza** are the result of juxtaposing seemingly divergent forms: some are closed, others fluid; orthogonal axes that yield to subtle shifts; the skilful use of an inclined plane of roofs and ramps; the free-standing steps of his monumental staircases; unusual and elegant objects deposited like archeological relics in the spaces of his interiors.

Faculty of Arts | Theo Bosch

Friedrichstadt Housing Block | Aldo Rossi

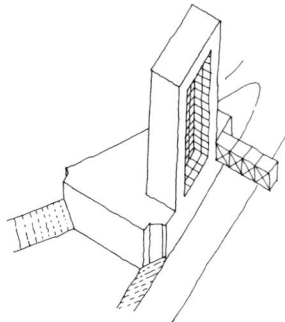

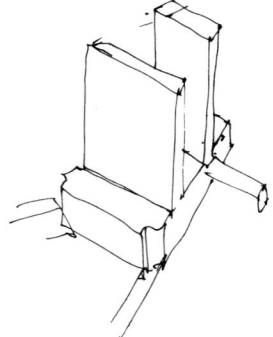

The references to **Le Corbusier**, **Loos**, **Aalto**, **Neutra** or **Mies van der Rohe** readily discernible in his buildings, are not direct architectural quotations made in complicity or tongue in cheek by someone who has done with the figurative culture of our modern age. On the contrary, they are the result of a transformation.

What is special about its architectonic sensibility is the way the reminders of modern architecture and the location are made the fragile fabric of the work's generative basis. This is far-removed from the imitative principle that guided the classical approach to architecture and it has nothing to do with innovation, nor today's obsession with innovation as the true aesthetic content. The transformation which these elements have undergone is an intellectual process which seeks significance in the very ambiguity that the process of continual reappraisal under changing conditions produces.

In his *'Eupalinos'*, **Paul Valéry** raises the question of the ambiguous nature, the *objet ambigu*, of modern architecture. He does not mean a contrived ambiguity, but one that proceeds from contemporary civilisation. The architectural creation, including **Siza's**, is not something that is fabricated, but, as **Valéry** states in his brilliant analysis of **Leonardo da Vinci's** methods, it is more like an *insight laboriously gleaned from the process of art*. In short then, it is intellectual emotion combined with specific, concrete, constructed materiality, albeit with a delicacy and dash of scepticism such as to be found in the buildings of **Alvaro Siza**.

Ignasi de Solà-Morales

National Museum of Roman Art |
Rafael Moneo

Musée d'Orsay | Gae Aulenti

Nominees for the Mies van der Rohe Award for European Architecture

Gae Aulenti
Musée d'Orsay, Paris, France 1980-1986

Theo Bosch
Faculty of Arts, Amsterdam, The Netherlands 1981-1984

Mario Botta
André Malraux Cultural Centre, Chambéry-le-Bas, France 1982-1987

Santiago Calatrava
Bach de Roda / Felip II Bridge, Barcelona, Spain 1987

Henri Ciriani
Hospital Kitchen, Paris, France 1981-1985

Alan Colquhoun / John Miller
Whitechapel Art Gallery, London, England 1984-1985

Norman Foster
Renault Centre, Swindon, England 1983

Henri Gaudin
Housing Block, Rue de Ménilmontant, Paris, France 1987

Herman Hertzberger
Haarlemmer Houttuinen Housing, Amsterdam, The Netherlands 1978-1982

Wilhelm Holzbauer
City Hall and Opera House, Amsterdam, The Netherlands 1982-1988

Josep Martorell / Oriol Bohigas / David Mackay
Creueta del Coll Park, Barcelona, Spain 1987

Rafael Moneo

National Museum of Roman Art, Mérida, Spain 1980-1986

Adolfo Natalini

Bank, Alzate Brianza, Italy 1983-1984

Jean Nouvel

Arab Cultural Centre, Paris, France 1987

Gustav Peichl

Phosphate Elimination Plant, Tegel-Berlin, West Germany 1985

Renzo Piano

Schlumberger Factories, Montrouge-Paris, France 1980-1985

Richard Rogers

Lloyd's of London, London, England 1981-1986

Aldo Rossi

Friedrichstadt Housing Block, Berlin, West Germany 1985-1987

Alvaro Siza

Borges & Irmão Bank, Vila do Conde, Portugal 1982-1986

Alcino Soutinho

City Hall, Matosinhos, Portugal 1983-1987

James Stirling

Clore Gallery, London, England 1982-1987

Oswald Mathias Ungers

Gatehouse, Frankfurt am Main, West Germany 1983-1986

Gino Valle

Housing on Giudecca, Venice, Italy 1980-1986

Francesco Venezia

Museum, Gibellina, Italy 1981-1987

Musée d'Orsay | Paris, France | 1980-1986

Gae Aulenti

In December 1986 the Musée d'Orsay opened its doors. The museum is housed in a railway station specially converted for the purpose and brings together works which were once dispersed between the Louvre, the old Palais du Luxembourg and the Jeu de Paume. It now gives unity to a collection ranging from 1848 to 1914.

The railway station and its adjacent hotel and restaurant were designed by **Victor Laloux** and inaugurated for the 1900 Universal Exhibition on July 14th. The buildings were situated on the Quai Anatole France on the left bank of the Seine in front of the Tuileries Gardens. By 1939, trains had become too long for the station's platforms, and it had to be closed. The main hall suffered various indignities before being finally abandoned. The outcry over the destruction of Les Halles focused attention on 19th-century architecture. In 1973 the railway station with its hotel and restaurant was acknowledged as a building of historic interest and a proposal to preserve it as a 19th-Century Art and French Civilisation Museum was approved. In 1978 a competition was held and designs invited for the conversion of the former station into a museum. It was won by the **ACT** Architecture team. Their project shifted the principal entrance from the long quay side to the more sheltered Rue Bellechasse. Inside, the hall became a street, flanked on both sides by exhibition galleries.

In 1980 programme revisions led to the appointment of the Milanese architect **Gae Aulenti** to design the interior architecture, lighting and museum furnishings. **Aulenti** accepted **ACT's** basic plans, but rejected their interior design, which was in an Art Deco-inspired style evoking associations with the luxury of the fin-de-siècle. For **Aulenti**, however, the building was *a free space calling for new and strong initiatives*. She therefore opted for an architecture without references to the railway station or to the period in which it was built. In fact her design strongly contrasts with the existing building and emphasizes the division between the existing and the new elements. Her choices include stone facings for the gallery walls and floors, an assertive colour scheme and, most importantly, temple-like galleries. In **Aulenti's** design the visitor's path became a circuit of typical museum-like spaces, such as rooms, galleries, passages and loggias.

Entering the Musée d'Orsay, the visitor is overwhelmed by the huge hall of

1927 Born in Palazzolo dello Stella, Udine, Italy.
1954 Graduated from the School of Architecture, Milan Polytechnic, Italy.
1955-1965 Editor of 'Casabella-Continuita'.
1960-1962 Assistant Professor of Architectural Composition, Faculty of Architecture, University of Venice, Italy.
1964 Grand International Prize for the Italian Pavilion at the XIII Triennale of Milan, Italy.
1966 Collaboration with Olivetti Company.
1968 Collaboration with Fiat Car Firm.
1969-1975 Visiting Lecturer, College of Architecture, Barcelona, Spain.
Visiting Lecturer, Cultural Centre, Stockholm, Sweden.
1976-1979 Worked in the 'Laboratorio di Progettazione Teatrale', Prato, Italy.
1980 'Ubu Prize' for best Italian stage design, Milan, Italy.
1983 Awarded the 'Medal of Architecture' by the Academy of Architecture, Paris, France.
1984 Awarded the 'Josef Hoffmann 1983 Prize' by the Academy of Applied Arts, Vienna, Austria.
1987 Chevalier de la Légion d'Honneur.
1987 Commandeur dans l'Ordre des Arts et Lettres.
1989 Awarded the Special Prize for Culture by the Presi-

dent of the 'Consiglio dei Ministri' of Italy.
Honorary Member of the American Society of Interior Designers (A.S.I.D.).
Honorary Member of the Association of German Architects (B.D.A.).

Major Works
1980-1986 Conversion of the Musée d'Orsay, Paris, France.
1985 Conversion of the National Palace of Montjuïc, Barcelona, Spain.
1986 Conversion of the Grassi Palace, Venice, Italy (in collaboration with A. Forcari).

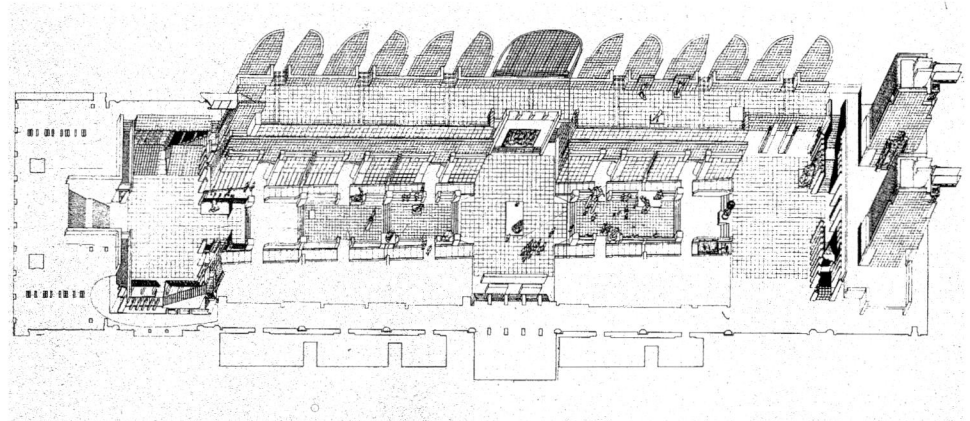

metal and glass. The entrance is situated on a higher level so the visitor has to descend a staircase to reach the street with the sculpture and paintings displays. The street is not inclined, as in the design of **ACT**, but consists of a succession of terraces sloping upwards and connected by steps.

The street is flanked by the temple-like galleries. Romanticism and its academic successors on one side face Realism to **Manet** on the other. One of the galleries provides access to a mezzanine floor with oval rooms overlooking the Seine and rooms on the Rue de Lille. At the east of the hall, two towers were designed as a new architectural form for the display of scale models and other objects.

In the eastern *Pavillon Amont* a freestanding elevator shaft is used to display an assembly of 19th-century architectural details. The space under the elevator is dedicated to **Charles Garnier's** Opéra, a model of which is seen through the *transparent* floor.

In the attic, situated above the oval rooms, the *Galerie des Hauteurs* displays the Impressionists. The *Café des Hauteurs,* with a terrace overlooking the Tuileries Gardens, marks the end of the gallery of the Impressionists. Beyond the cafeteria, the *Galerie Bellechasse* displays post-Impressionist works. This gallery's colonnade recalls the layout of corridors and rooms in the hotel. The descent to the ground floor leads through the *Passage de Presse,* where newspaper excerpts place the art in its historical context.

Musée d'Orsay | Gae Aulenti

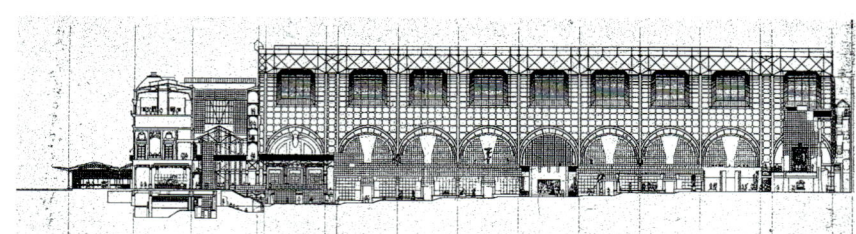

In 1976 the University of Amsterdam commissioned the architectural office of **Van Eyck** and **Bosch** to prepare designs for a new building. It was **Theo Bosch** who actually designed the building. The Faculty of Arts, situated in the heart of the city, extends along a whole block overlooking the Singel canal. The building absorbs the rehabilitated old buildings at either end, taking its colour scheme from that on the right, the *White House,* designed in 1899 by the brothers **J. and C. Verheul**. It was saved from demolition and converted for the use of the Faculty. The low-rise buildings in Torensteeg were also retained. This was one of the conditions the architect made before accepting the commission. Other requirements were that at least some of the ground floor be given over to public use (shops and a pedestrian passage) and that the roof be used for terraces at several levels. The building volume is split up into *repeatable units.* Their size is determined by the tutorial rooms, located on the third and fourth floors. They express the essence of education; a number of students gathered around a teacher. The tutorial rooms are deliberately arranged to be seen into from circulation routes so that students are familiar with everything that happens in the building. They are placed in a U-shape to create light wells and glass-enclosed seminar rooms on alternate sides. The effect is of light and transparency. In this way every room in the plan has natural light and views outside.

The third floor also includes a cafeteria with small terraces. The library is located on the first and second floor. The library levels are connected by two sorts of well. Some, overlooking the canal, are set against the external skin and allow side light deep into the plan. Other wells are more central and are lit from above by roof lights in the floor of the light courts. The first floor also contains lecture theatres, which are broad and shallow in plan with glazed rear walls. Below that, on the ground floor, are various language laboratories, shops and a passage. The basement contains recreation areas.

This arrangement is based on the form of a pyramid. The large, general spaces, such as the entrance hall, library and cafeteria are situated on the lower levels. These are the most intensively used areas. The tutorial rooms and staff-rooms are more suited to the upper floors. **Theo Bosch** has

1940 Born in Amsterdam, The Netherlands.

1956 Junior Secondary Technical School; carpentry and furniture-making.

1956-1959 Evening classes, Higher Technical School.

1963-1970 Studied at the Academy of Architecture, Amsterdam, The Netherlands.

Until 1965 worked in several architects' offices.

1965-1971 Assistant in the office of Aldo van Eyck, Amsterdam, The Netherlands.

1971-1982 Partnership with Aldo van Eyck.

1984 Started an architectural office.

1984 Awarded the Wibaut Award by the City of Amsterdam, The Netherlands.

Since 1987 Chairman of the Building Regulations Committee, The Hague, The Netherlands.

1989 Concrete-Use Award.

1989 Vision '89 Award.

1990 Visiting Lecturer, Academy of Arts, Hamburg, West Germany.

Lectured at the Academy of Architecture, Amsterdam, The Netherlands.

Lectured at the Academy of Arts, Berlin, West Germany

Major works

Many housing projects in Amsterdam.

1981-1984 Faculty of Arts, University of Amsterdam, The Netherlands.

1987-1988 Sijzenbaan housing complex, Deventer, The Netherlands.

Theo Bosch

Faculty of Arts | Amsterdam, The Netherlands | 1981-1984

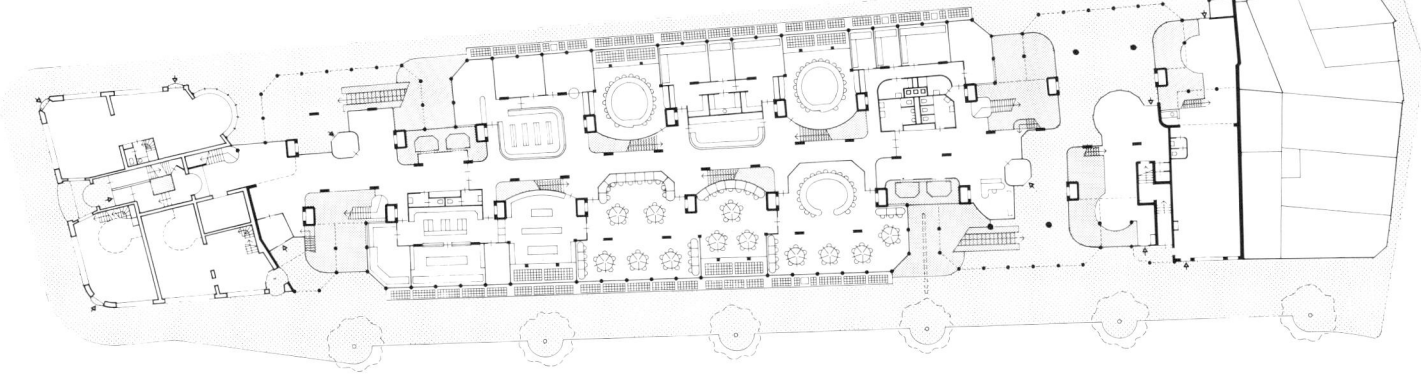

exploited this pyramidal factor in a very particular way. He has solved the vertical reduction in use-intensity on plan and elevation rather than in section. The indentations which allow light deep into the building cause the useful floor area of the upper floor to be reduced. The staggering of the basic units gives rise to sections in the form of half-pyramids one behind the other, whose sloping sides face alternately left and right. This form is, however, only visible at the indentations themselves and these are extra narrow because the staff-rooms are curled round them.

The outside of the building appears to consist of a number of office towers. The pyramidal form is also expressed in their unequal heights. The towers are given added emphasis by the liberal use of bay-windows and balustrading, which together create a varying rhythm in the elevations and thus relates them to the existing buildings, especially the *White House,* whose dimensions are related to those of the towers.

Bosch wanted the faculty building to demonstrate the ideal of a *chaotic city.* It attracts students, teachers and visitors to the heart of the city. Their presence can be seen as an investment in the life of the city. The central corridor can be compared with an internal street, and the recreation areas in the basement, which can be seen from outside the building as well as from the inside, are comparable with squares.

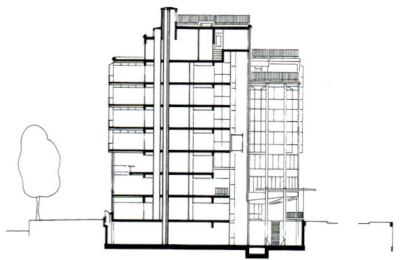

Faculty of Arts | Theo Bosch

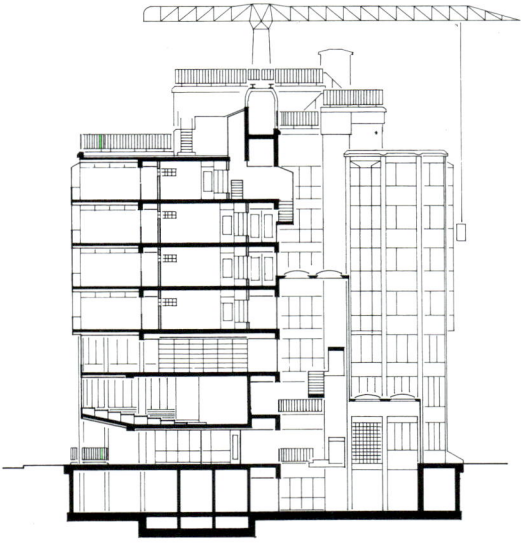

André Malraux Cultural Centre | Chambéry-le-Bas, France | 1982-1987

Mario Botta

The part of Chambéry in which the **André Malraux** Cultural Centre is situated was dominated, until 1980, by the presence of large military buildings. The municipal authorities decided to demolish some of them in order to convert the area to collective use. Two commissions were awarded for the barracks area and a competition by invitation was advertised for a theatre project. **Henri Ciriani** designed a residential complex and **Jean-Patrick Fortier** submitted a scheme for the re-use of the former Curial barracks, the only structure left after the other military buildings had been demolished. **Mario Botta** won the competition for the theatre. Only his building and the complete renovation of the Curial barracks by **Fortier** have been realised. The residential complex designed by **Ciriani** was abandoned after the foundations were laid.

The André Malraux Cultural Centre was intended to be the focus of a renewed cultural and residential district, located just outside the medieval centre of the city. In **Mario Botta's** design, the wide courtyard of the Curial barracks, which date from the Napoleonic era, now serves as an open foyer for theatre-goers. The east wing of the barracks has been adapted to contain the entrance hall, rehearsal rooms, meeting rooms, a gallery, a cafeteria, offices and other public areas.

The theatre visitors enter the cultural centre through the barracks courtyard and pass from the old to the new bulding by a glazed bridge which offers a view of the surrounding urban area. The 950-seat theatre and the cinema below it occupy a striking half-cylinder, while the stage and fly tower, rehearsal and dressing rooms fill an imposing block that towers over the half-cylinder and three-storey barracks. *The new architectural element is seen as a large curved surface that emphasises the barracks' east side, while at the same time affirming its own presence and functional autonomy.*

Botta's paired volumes face one another like two compact bodies, distinguished on one side by the theatre's emergency stairs, which start at the north-east edge of the cylinder, defining a secluded plaza between the barracks and the theatre. This small square establishes a new relationship between the fabric of the historic city and the presence of the André Malraux Cultural Centre. Also on this side, the stone and concrete facade is cut with a jagged edge to reveal the interior stairs and glazed foyers, which

1943 Born in Mendrisio, Switzerland.
1961-1964 Studied at Milan Art College, Italy.
1964-1969 Studied at the School of Architecture, University of Venice, Italy.
1965 Assistant in the office of Le Corbusier in Venice and Paris.
1969 Started an architectural office in Lugano, Switzerland.
1976, 1980, 1982 Visiting Professor, Federal Polytechnic, Lausanne, Switzerland.
1983 Professor, Federal Polytechnic, Lausanne, Switzerland.
1985 Beton Prize for Architecture.
1986 Chicago Architecture Award.
1987 Visiting Professor, School of Architecture, Yale University, New Haven, U.S.A.
1989 The Royal Dutch Brick Organisation's 'Baksteen' Award, The Netherlands.
1989 Awarded the C.I.C.A. Award by the InternationaL Committee of Architectural Critics, Buenos Aires, Argentina.
1989 Honorary Professor, Escuela de Altos Estudios del C.A.Y.C., Buenos Aires, Argentina.

Honorary Fellow of the Association of German Architects (B.D.A.).
Honorary Fellow of the American Institute of Architects (A.I.A.).

Major works
1981 Single-family house (Casa Rotonda), Stabio, Switzerland.
1977-1981 State bank, Fribourg, Switzerland.
1982-1987 André Malraux Cultural Centre, Chambéry, France.
1986-1987 Library, Villeurbanne, France.

L. Fontana e A. Mensa per Mario Botta

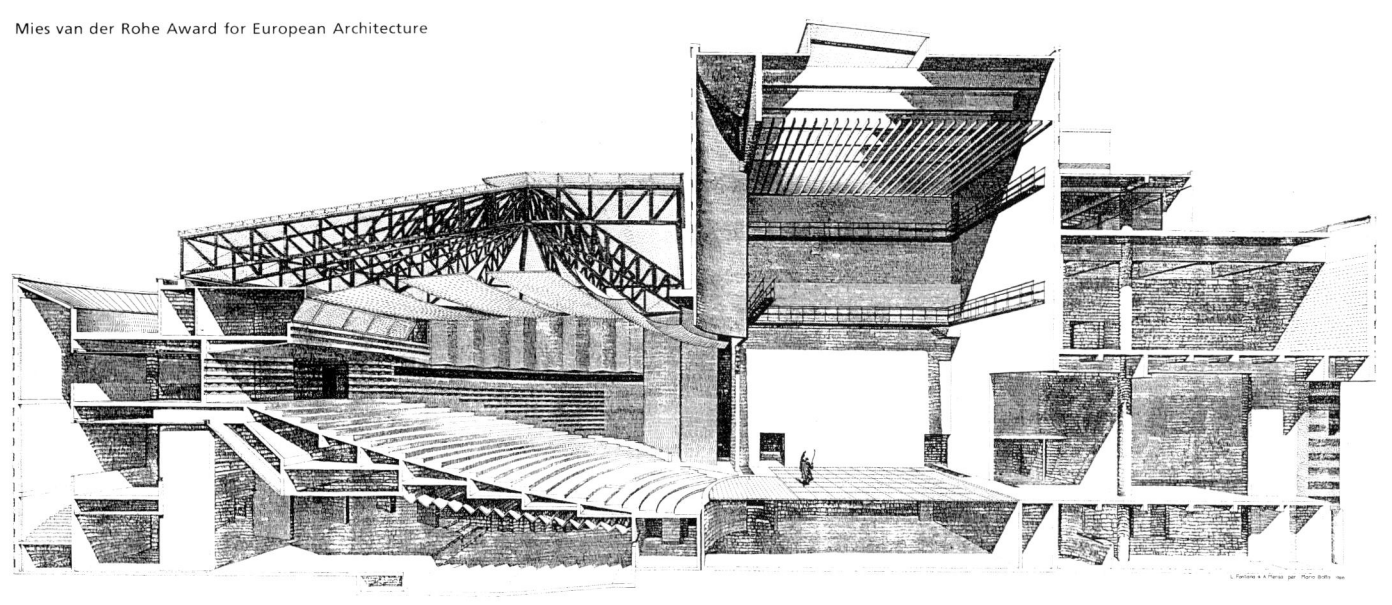

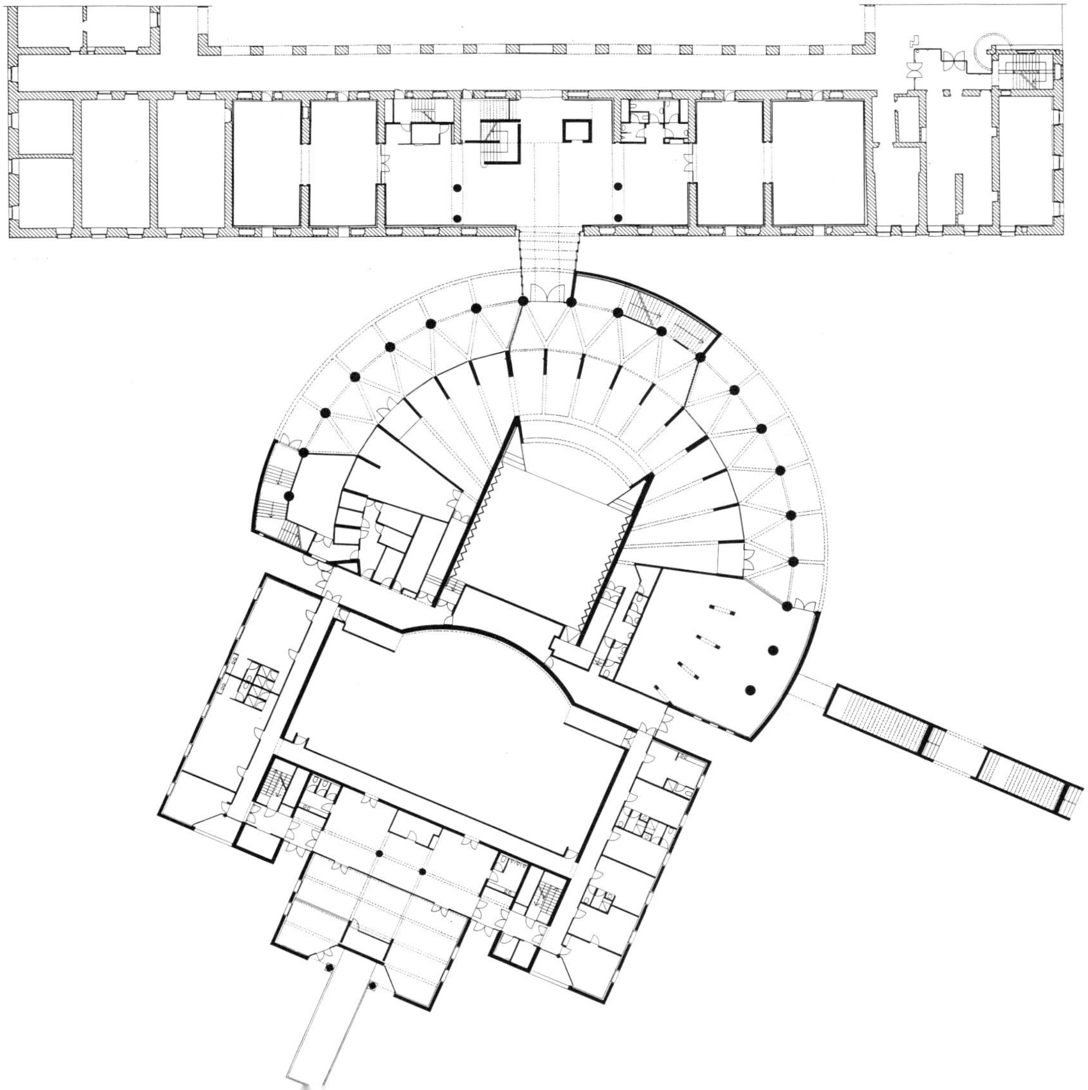

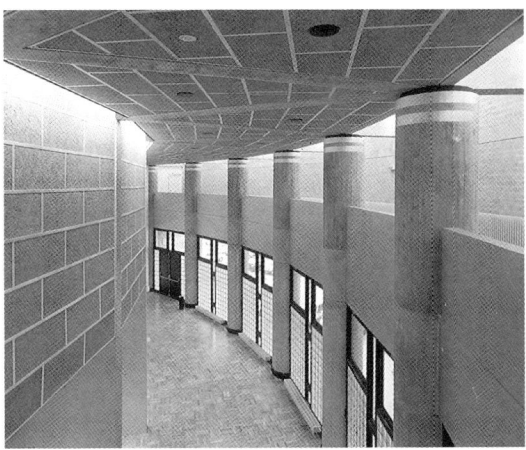

wrap around the ground-floor cinema and theatre seating one flight up. The interplay of light and mass is everywhere. The function of the building is clearly legible in its layout and the treatment of the different spaces. Although **Botta** had originally positioned the theatre perpendicular to the Curial barracks, it was later shifted to align with the existing grid of the city. The theatre's striations of concrete and limestone recall the Romanesque churches that served as **Botta's** inspiration. The heavy walls have no conventional windows but instead are pierced by narrow slits that recall medieval fortresses. These openings, together with the use of primary volumes, each serving a distinct function, and the striated compositions of stone, concrete and glass are characteristic of **Botta's** work. The striped exterior facades are echoed in the public foyer and within the theatre itself in alternating grey and yellow bands of stone and wood.

André Malraux Cultural Centre | Mario Botta

Bach de Roda / Felip II Bridge | Barcelona, Spain | 1987

Santiago Calatrava

The Barcelona bridge, designed by the engineer and architect **Santiago Calatrava**, was conceived as part of a scheme for the reorganisation of an extensive area in central Barcelona which was on the edge of the urban area devised by the Cerdà Plan and spanned the railway lines coming in from the north. In this redevelopment scheme two major interventions were envisaged: the creation of a large park alongside the railway and the linking up of Felip II and Bach de Roda streets. These were separated by the railway and by linking them up the bridge provides direct access to the sea. At the same time the bridge can be seen as a *major sculptural feature* in the urban landscape. This effect is achieved mainly by the large arches, from which the structure of the risers is suspended. As well as giving the bridge a monumental appearance, these arches make it recognizable even from a distance. The supports for the reinforced concrete bridge also appear to be carved out of a single block of stone and shaped by the hand of a sculptor. Because of its sculptural qualities, the bridge fits very naturally into the urban landscape.

The bridge has an overall length of 128 metres and is divided into three sections: the middle section spanning the railway is 45 metres long and the two lateral sections are each 25 metres long. They cross the fringes of the park without disturbing its users. The two lateral sections constitute the longitudinal structural elements of the bridge and have a box girder section with a static depth of 1.80 metres. The middle section consists of a series of steel girders resting on both sides. The roadway is made up of a grid of transverse steel girders on top of which is set a 20 cm-thick slab of concrete, thereby forming a monolithic ensemble of slab and girder that is capable of absorbing the vertical stresses caused by the passage of road traffic.

The two pairs of arches widen slightly at both ends, increasing structural rigidity and permitting the passage of pedestrians on footpaths to either side of the bridge. Four flights of steps, two from each side of the bridge, follow the line of the arches and link up the two edges of the park (divided by the railway) with the pavements of the bridge. The stairs also have structural functions in supporting the inclined arch and the bridge. The twin arches define a central space which is accentuated by the lateral surfaces, since they are not flat but slightly concave, so creating two suspended

1951 Born in Valencia, Spain.
1968-1969 Studied at Valencia Art School, Spain.
1969-1973 Studied at the School of Architecture, Valencia, Spain.
1975-1979 Studied Civil Engineering at the Federal Polytechnic, Zürich, Switzerland.
1979-1981 Assistant, Federal Polytechnic, Zürich, Switzerland.
1981 Started an architectural and civil engineering office in Zürich, Switzerland.
1987 August Perret Prize.
1988 City of Barcelona Prize, Spain.
1988 Fritz Schumacher Prize, West Germany.
1988 F.A.D. Prize, Spain.
1988 Fazlur Rahman Khan International Fellowship for Architecture and Engineering.

Member of the Association of Swiss Architects (B.S.A.).
Member of the International Academy of Architecture.

Major works
1987 Television studio, Zürich, Switzerland.
1987 Bach de Roda/Felip II Bridge, Barcelona, Spain.
1988 Footbridge, Paris, France.
1989 9 de Octubre Motorway Bridge, Valencia, Spain.

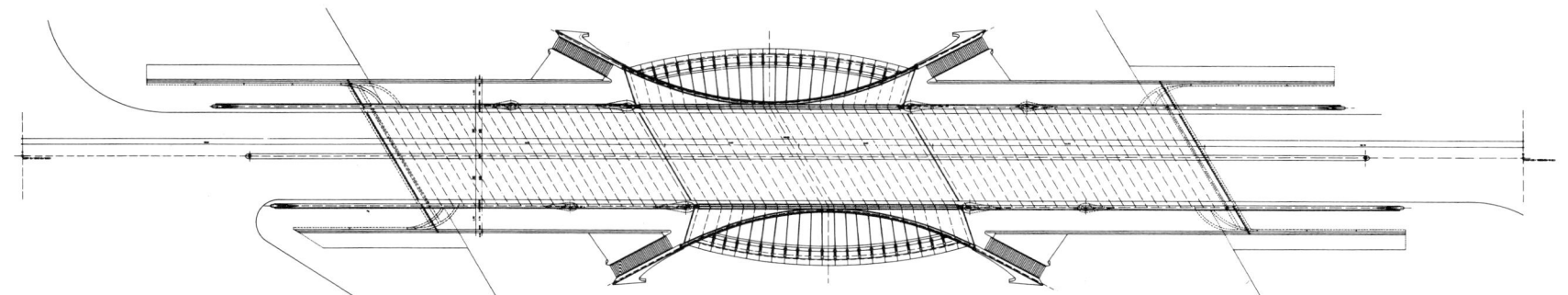

plazas linked to the park by the lateral staircases.

The middle section, formed out of an arched girder, is connected to the bridge girder by tie-beams. The arches form the structural continuation of the concrete lateral wing, the stairs, and at the top reach as far as the arch girders in the strict sense. All the arches are made out of 2 or 3 cm-thick steel plate and have a box section.

The bridge has three types of bearing: abutments, intermediate bearings and central bearings. The abutments of the bridge are formed by a containing wall of unplastered concrete of varying height. The intermediate bearings consist of truncated conical elements about 4 metres in height and made of unplastered concrete. Their function is to transmit vertical forces to the foundations and to take up, along with the lateral wings, the horizontal forces. The central bearings are designed as pendular supports and work by pure compression. They consist of two monolithic columns of solid granite housed at the ends in concrete.

Bach de Roda / Felip II Bridge | Santiago Calatrava

The kitchen of the St. Antoine Hospital is located in Rue de Citeaux in Paris' twelfth *arrondissement*. Like all hospitals built over a period of 100 years, it has developed by accretion. The site for the new kitchen was a residual space on the north side of Rue de Citeaux. To one side was a tall building on the scale typical of a Paris street, to the other a two-storey neo-classical building belonging to the hospital to which a third floor had been added. The context was urban infill, with the additional task of mediating between the different scales of the two adjacent buildings. The building plot was approximately 30 metres square and all access, vehicular and pedestrian, was from the rear. With no need for access from the street, **Ciriani** had the opportunity to highlight the formal question of the facade.

The design of the building is based on a *cube*. The plan was to anchor one corner of the plot, liberating the rest of the space. The problem of mediating between a tall neighbour on one side and a much lower building on the other has been solved by a progression from high to low. The air extraction plant is designed to attain the necessary height to the left. The extractors are located over an open area of the plan and are vented against the higher building. So the air exhaust system is taken right across the facade to the plant tower at the corner.

The most striking feature is the *spatial transparency* of the building. It is always seen in silhouette, because the sun is always behind it. The requirement for height is met by delicate framing, rather than a solid volume. The street is not denied its sunshine, since the light penetrates the open frame. The sun also reaches into the building by means of a series of roof lights on the garden terraces. As the height of the building increases, the sun penetrates the various levels and at the top it pours through into the street.

The ground floor accommodates a large central space for the preparation of food. There is a distinction between the service areas, such as rooms for storage, preparation and cooking, and the served areas where the distribution of the meals takes place. The service areas form a wall which marks off two sides of the free plan to contain the space in which the meals are dished up. This served area opens up on a diagonal towards the hospital and the sun. Pedestrian traffic from the hospital is directed around the loading bays off to one side which define the edge of the kitchen site. This

50

1936 Born in Lima, Peru.
1960 Graduated from the National University of Architecture, Lima, Peru.
1962-1964 Assistant Professor, National University of Architecture, Lima, Peru.
1964 Settled in Paris, France.
1968-1982 Member of the Atelier of Urbanism and Architecture (A.U.A.), Bagnolet, France.
1976 Started an architectural office in Paris, France.
1983 Grand Prix Nationale d'Architecture.
1984 Silver Square Award.
1984 Visiting Critic, Tulane University, New Orleans, U.S.A.
1984 Visiting Critic, the Department of Architecture, the Polytechnic of Plymouth, England.
1985 Distinguished Professor, National University of Architecture, Lima, Peru.
1985 Visiting Professor, University of Dublin, Ireland.
1987 Visiting Professor, University College, University of London, England.
1987 Visiting Critic, Columbia University Graduate School of Architectural Planning and Preservation, New York, U.S.A.
1988 Palme d'Or Nationale.

Major works
1981-1985 St. Antoine Hospital Kitchen, Paris, France.
1982 'La Cour d'Angle' housing, St. Denis, Paris, France.
1983 'La Cour d'Angle' crèche, St Denis, Paris, France.

Henri Ciriani

Hospital Kitchen | Paris, France | 1981-1985

51

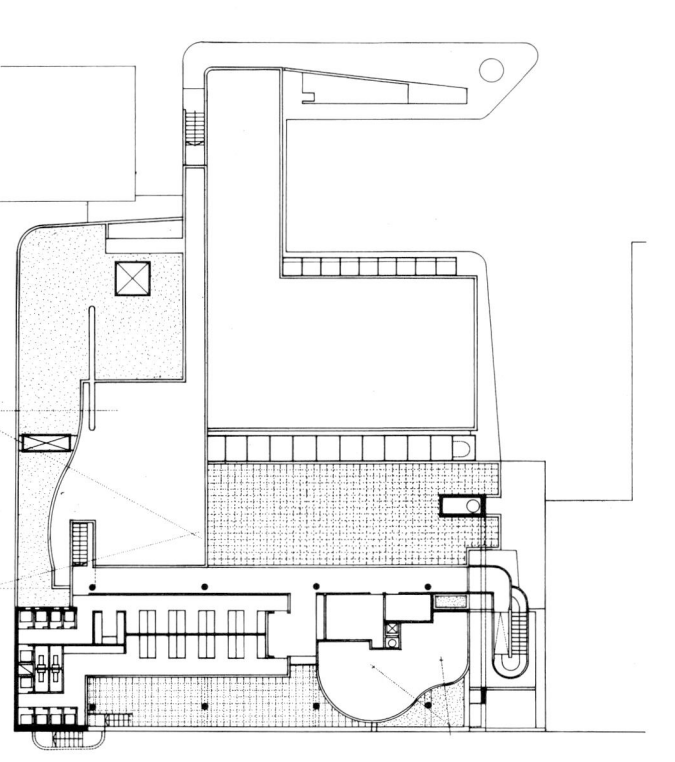

sets up the route through the kitchen. Some of the hospital's territory is appropriated by this promenade, since it begins as people approach the kitchen from the hospital grounds.

The first floor accommodates an entrance, office, changing rooms, recreation space and a loggia-like tambour, all intended for the kitchen staff. From the tambour one can enjoy a panoramic view. The free forms and particularly the glass-brick tambour clearly stand out against the sky.

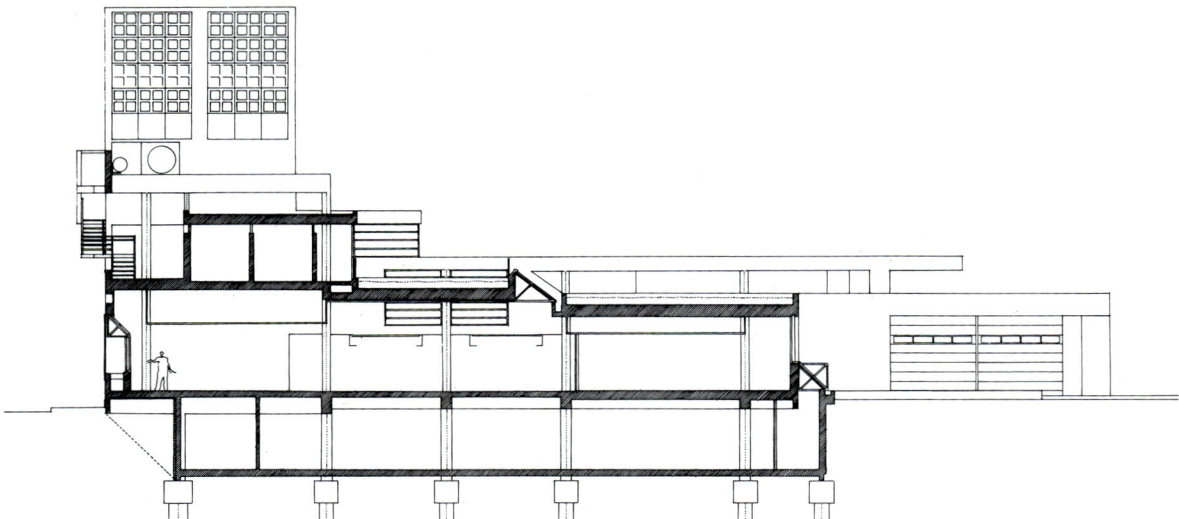

Hospital Kitchen | Henri Ciriani

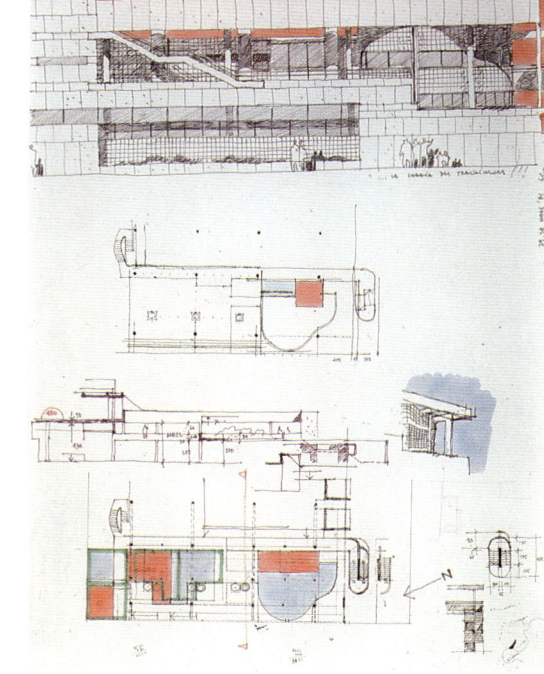

Whitechapel Art Gallery | London, England | 1984-1985

Alan Colquhoun, John Miller

The Whitechapel Art Gallery in London's East End dates from 1901 and was designed by **Charles Harrison Townsend**. The modern art gallery has become a much more complex type of organisation than it was at the turn of the century. Not only does it require a larger curatorial staff and an increase in ancillary accommodation, both public and infrastructural, but modern standards of picture preservation and human comfort demand a much more sophisticated system of environmental control than was necessary in the past. All these requirements demanded that the building was to be more or less *radically transformed*. **Colquhoun** and **Miller** were asked to make alterations and additions to the Whitechapel Art Gallery. There were two major constraints to do with preservation. First, **Townsend's** facade could not be altered, except to remove two attic windows inserted into what was to have been a painted frieze. Second, the client and the Greater London Council wanted the main galleries to be left intact as far as possible.

A plot of land adjoining the gallery was acquired and could be used to solve some of the problems. This enabled the architects not only to build new accommodation on the newly acquired land, but also to reorganise the accommodation within the existing building to create more space. The architects were instructed to improve the existing galleries and office space and to add a new gallery. They also had to provide extra storage, loading facilities, preparation spaces, a freight elevator, new lecture and education spaces, a new book store, a larger cafeteria and alternative access to each gallery level, so that one part could be used while the other was being prepared for a new exhibition.

These new elements had to be provided either within the existing building envelope or in the new extension occupying a narrow strip of land in Angel Alley. The existing school building in the alley had to be demolished and a new five-storey structure, sharing a long party-wall with the existing gallery, was erected. The most important internal alterations, affecting the public use of the two existing galleries, are the two new staircases. One provides a visually apparent public access to the first-floor gallery from the foyer. The other, a long continuous flight, broken only by a lobby to the cafeteria, leads to the far end of the upper gallery via a new gallery on the first floor. Both staircases replace existing staircases enclosed in a brick structure. The

1921 Born in the United Kingdom.
1939-1942 Studied at the Edinburgh College of Art, Scotland.
1949 Graduated from the Architectural Association, London, England.
1957-1964 Tutor, Architectural Association, London, England.
Since 1961 Partnership with John Miller.
1966, 1968, 1970 Visiting Lecturer, Princeton University, New Jersey, U.S.A.
1968, 1971 Visiting Lecturer, Cornell University, Ithaca, New York, U.S.A.
1974 Senior Lecturer, The Polytechnic of Central London, England.
1976-1978 Principal Lecturer, the Polytechnic of Central London, England.
1977 Visiting Professor, Federal Polytechnic, Lausanne, Switzerland.
1978 Visiting Lecturer, Princeton University, New Jersey, U.S.A.
Since 1978 Professor of Architecture, Princeton University, New Jersey, U.S.A.
1985 Resident in Architecture, American Academy, Rome, Italy.
1988 R.I.B.A. Regional Architecture Award, Whitechapel Art Gallery, London, England.

Associate of the Royal Institute of British Architects, (R.I.B.A.).

1930 Born in London, England.
1957 Graduated from the Architectural Association, London, England.
1959-1961 Assistant to Sir Leslie Martin, Cambridge, England.
Since 1961 Partnership with Alan Colquhoun.
1961-1973 Tutor, Interior and Environmental Design School, Royal College of Art, London, England.
1966-1968 Visiting Critic, Cornell University, Ithaca, New York, U.S.A.
1970 Visiting Critic, Princeton University School of Architecture, New Jersey, U.S.A.
1972-1973 Visiting Critic, Dublin University School of Architecture, Ireland.
1975-1985 Professor, Interior and Environmental Design School, Royal College of Art, London, England.
1985-1986 Visiting Professor, Dublin University School of Architecture, Ireland.
Since 1986 Visiting Professor, School of Architecture, University of Manchester, England.
1988 R.I.B.A. Regional Architecture Award, Whitechapel Art Gallery, London, England.

Associate of the Royal Institute of British Architects (R.I.B.A.).
Fellow of the Royal College of Art.

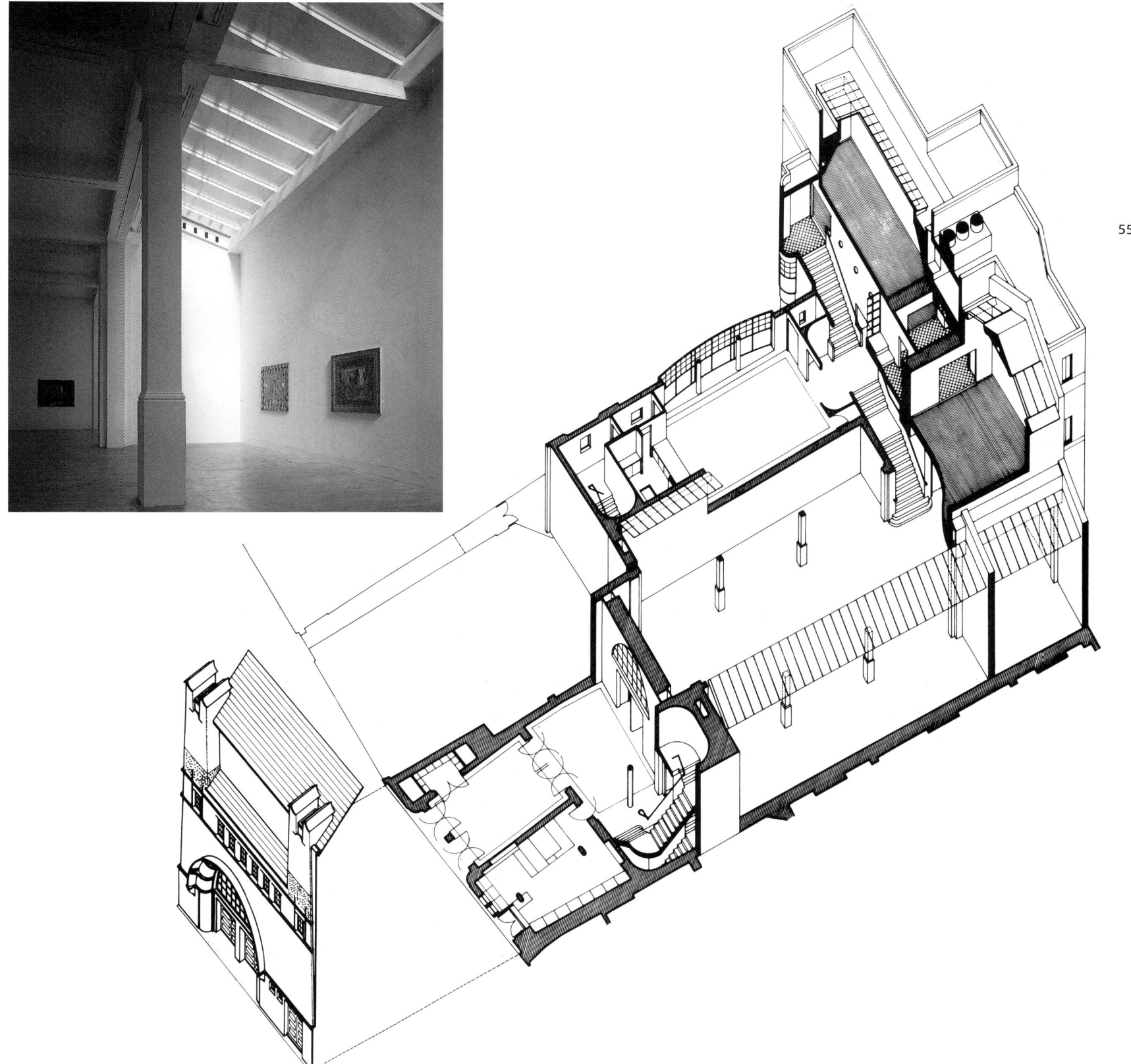

new staircases provide what was lacking in the original building: *a sense of spatial continuity between the ground floor and the first-floor galleries.*

The existing interiors are stylistically neutral. There are few clues as to the treatment of new elements, though certain motifs, such as roof lighting to the gallery and the entrance arch have been reinforced. The typical spaces in the old gallery have been maintained, while the linking spaces between and outside them have been completely transformed.

On Angel Alley a new facade and a secondary entrance to the gallery were created. This facade is not visible from the main road and is never in view at the same time as **Townsend's** facade.

The strategy adopted by **Colquhoun** and **Miller** in modifying this building was based, on the one hand, on the need to preserve all that was typical and, on the other, on the licence to invent new forms and in no way to copy the particular treatment that the **Townsend** building was given in the first instance.

Major works
1984-1985 Whitechapel Art Gallery, London, England.
1986 National Gallery extension, London, England.
1986 Royal College of Art faculty building, London, England.

56

Whitechapel Art Gallery | Alan Colquhoun, John Miller

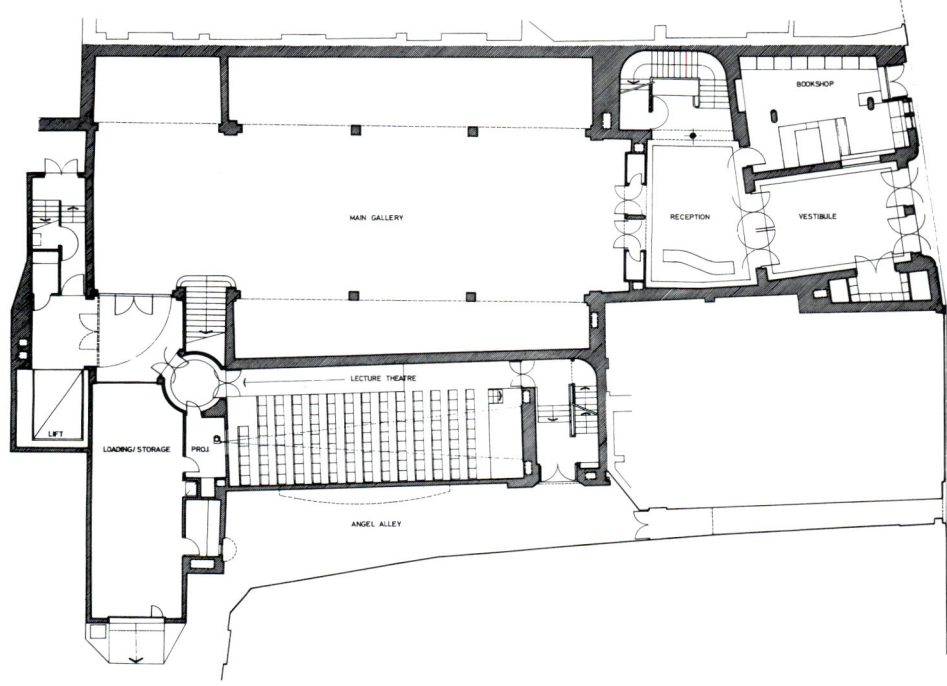

MAIN GALLERY

BOOKSHOP

RECEPTION

VESTIBULE

LECTURE THEATRE

LIFT

LOADING/ STORAGE   PROJ.

ANGEL ALLEY

Renault Centre | Swindon, England | 1983

Norman Foster

The Renault Centre is built on an irregular sloping plot of 6.5 hectares (approximately 16 acres) on the western edge of Swindon, a fast growing town of 127.000 people, in the South-West of England. The town is connected to London by a system of rapid road and rail links. At the outset of the project, Renault presented the challenge of establishing a progressive image of design quality which would extend out from their product range across to their working environments. This quest for excellence was to be sought within demanding limits of time and cost in ways which would also accommodate the dynamic of change during the building's life.

Foster's design concept integrated a response to both the site and the brief by using a module which could fill out the site irregularities with the potential for random growth in time. From the outside the building is articulated *by the scale of the individual modules, their expressed structures and a coordinating use of the Renault yellow house colour.* The Centre is organised in a series of 24-square-metres module, whose corners are defined by 16-metre-high tubular steel masts protruding through the roof to carry the tension rods from which hangs the undulating internal structure of the roof. This complex structure has great delicacy and variety in its individual parts. The first stage of construction comprised 42 modules, which accommodate a warehouse, distribution and regional offices with computer installations, a showroom for cars and trucks, an after-sales maintenance engineering training school with associated workshops and seminar rooms, a restaurant and entrance canopy. The grand interior of the warehouse is completely different from the small spaces of the training area beyond the big fire wall to the south. The showroom contains a semi-circular audiovisual auditorium with walls which can be made to descend from on high. The initial building ground plan can be expanded by 67%, the suspension structure providing connection points for this to be done without disruptive influences. The structural frame of the Renault Centre comprises arched steel beams which are suspended at quarter points from the top of pre-stressed, circular, rolled, hollow-steel masts. The floor construction is reinforced concrete with accurately levelled, monolithic, granolithic topping, on a sand-blasted slab base and heavy-duty polythene damp-proofing membrane. The roof cover consists of a continuous, solvent, welded, specially reinforced PVC mem-

1935 Born in Manchester, England.
1961 Graduated from Manchester University (Studies in Architecture and City Planning), England.
1961 Awarded a Henry Fellowship to Yale University, New Haven, U.S.A.
1961 Master's Degree in Architecture, Yale University, New Haven, U.S.A.
1963-1967 Partnership with Richard and Su Rogers and Wendy Foster in Team 4.
1967 Established 'Foster Associates' with Wendy Foster.
1968-1983 Worked with Buckminster Fuller on various projects.
1983 Royal Gold Medal for Architecture (R.I.B.A.).

Member of the Royal Institute of British Architects (R.I.B.A.). Associate of the Royal Academy of Arts, London, England. Honorary Fellow of the American Institute of Architects (A.I.A.).
Honorary Member of the Association of German Architects (B.D.A.).
Member of the French Order of Architects.

Major works
1971 Office building Fred Olsen Lines, London, England.
1975 Office building Willis, Faber & Dumas, Ipswich, England.
1978 Sainsbury Centre for Visual Arts, Norwich, England.
1983 Renault Centre, Swindon, England.
1986 Office building Hong Kong & Shanghai Bank, Hong Kong.

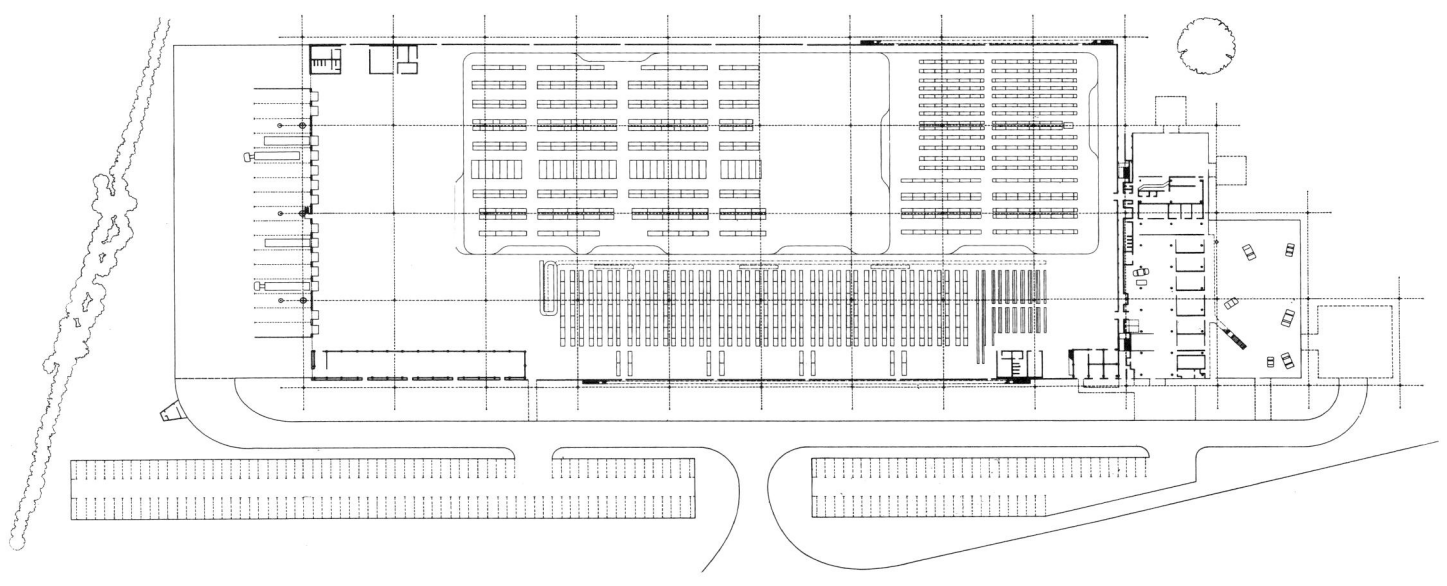

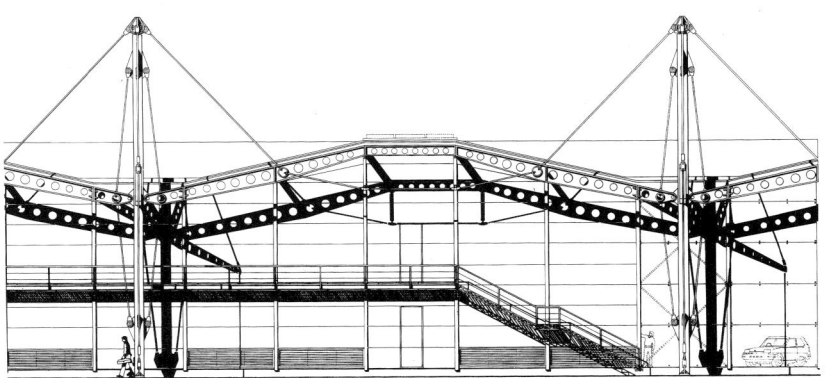

brane. A clear glass panel at each column combines the benefits of natural light with views of the structural masts and tension rods. At the apex of each module there is a further rooflight of double-skin, translucent PVC louvres, which can also be used for automatic smoke release or summer ventilation. The special external wall panels comprise expanded polyurethane foam insulation between two skins of steel. For glazing the wall and rooflights **Foster** used the Pilkington *Planar* system, an assembly of armour-plated glass suspended on bolts countersunk into the thickness of the glass. This method made it possible to mechanically 'pin' large glass plates to a main frame steel structure while accommodating both structural movement and erection tolerances. At the Renault Centre sheets of armour-plated glass, 4 metres long by 1.8 metres high, are held in place by eight 6 millimetre bolts.

The office, showroom and restaurant furniture is a combination of special systems designed by **Foster and Associates**. Some items were re-used from other Renault facilities.

Renault Centre | Norman Foster

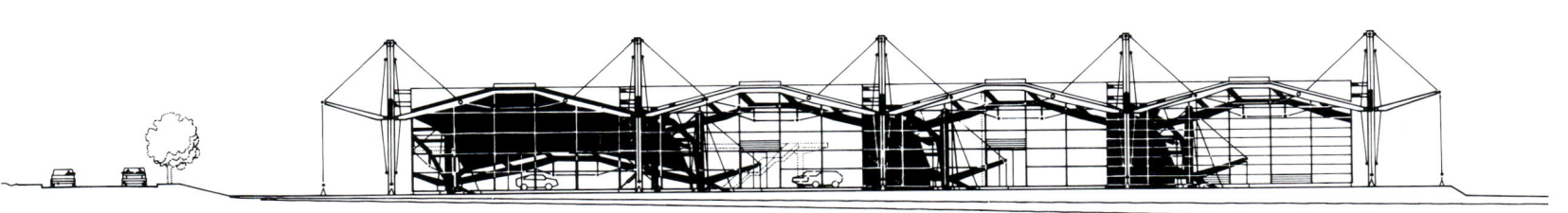

Rue de Ménilmontant is in the twentieth *arrondissement* of Paris, just north of the Père Lachaise cemetery. Here, at the corner of Rue Delaître, **Henri Gaudin** designed a block of 36 apartments on a narrow, almost rectangular site. Twelve three-room apartments take up the larger part of the building. There are also six two-room apartments, six with four rooms, two with five rooms and one with six rooms as well as nine studio apartments. On the ground floor there are two shops.

One striking aspect of the design is that **Gaudin** has not used all of the site for housing. He believes that a space should be left within a block which can develop as naturally as possible. His design was influenced by what he says is a typically Parisian lay out of houses built close together along the building lines with surprisingly deep courtyards and gardens behind reached by passages.

In the complex on Rue de Ménilmontant he created a large open space which crosses the site diagonally and serves as a courtyard for the residents. It is reached through an inconspicuous passage on the corner of Rue de Ménilmontant and Rue Delaître. This inner space shows that a city consists of more than just streets and facades. Both concealed and more visible elements determine the life of a city. An unobtrusive passage to a courtyard, as in Rue de Ménilmontant, reveals something of the complexity of the space within and makes the passer-by curious about what else there is to be seen.

The building has a ground floor and five storeys above. On Rue Delaître the height varies between three and four storeys. The facades have been given a sculptural treatment and suggest associations with a ship. On Rue Ménilmontant the undulating front evokes the afterdeck of a ship and it projects 60 cm forwards at various points. On Rue Delaître the facade deviates by 20 cm from the building line. This undulating form creates a lively play of light and shadow. At the corner of the two streets light and shadow again play an important part. Here the facade recedes at ground level, leaving a shaded area and making the corner less sharp. **Gaudin** believes it is important that the different parts of the building should give each other shade and colour. In his view a building should interact with other buildings rather than stand alone. It should reveal itself through reflections and shades of colour. **Gaudin** thinks of architecture as expression through volumes and details.

62

1933 Born in Paris, France.
1956-1966 Studied at the National University of Arts, Paris, France.
1964 Awarded First Prize by the American Architects of the Studio Laloux.
1964 Academy of Architecture Delors Foundation Prize.
1967-1969 Awarded the Delanoe-Aldrich Foundation Prize by the American Institute of Architects (A.I.A.).
1968-1969 Worked at the office of Harrison Abramovitch, New York, U.S.A.
1969-1973 Worked at the Parisian Office of Town Planning (A.P.U.R.).
1972-1976 Lecturer in Anthropology and Town Planning, University of Ethnology, Paris, France.
1981 Teacher, School of Architecture, Versailles, France.
1982 Member of the Board of Directors of the Le Corbusier Foundation.
1983 Academy of Architecture Silver Medal.
1986 Silver Square Award.

Major works
1981 Housing in Elancourt-Maurepas, France.
1985 Housing in Evry-Courcouronnes, France.
1987 Housing in Rue de Ménilmontant, Paris, France.
1987 Extension to the Tandou College, Paris, France.

Henri Gaudin

Housing Block, Rue de Ménilmontant | Paris, France | 1987

Housing Block, Rue de Ménilmontant | Henri Gaudin

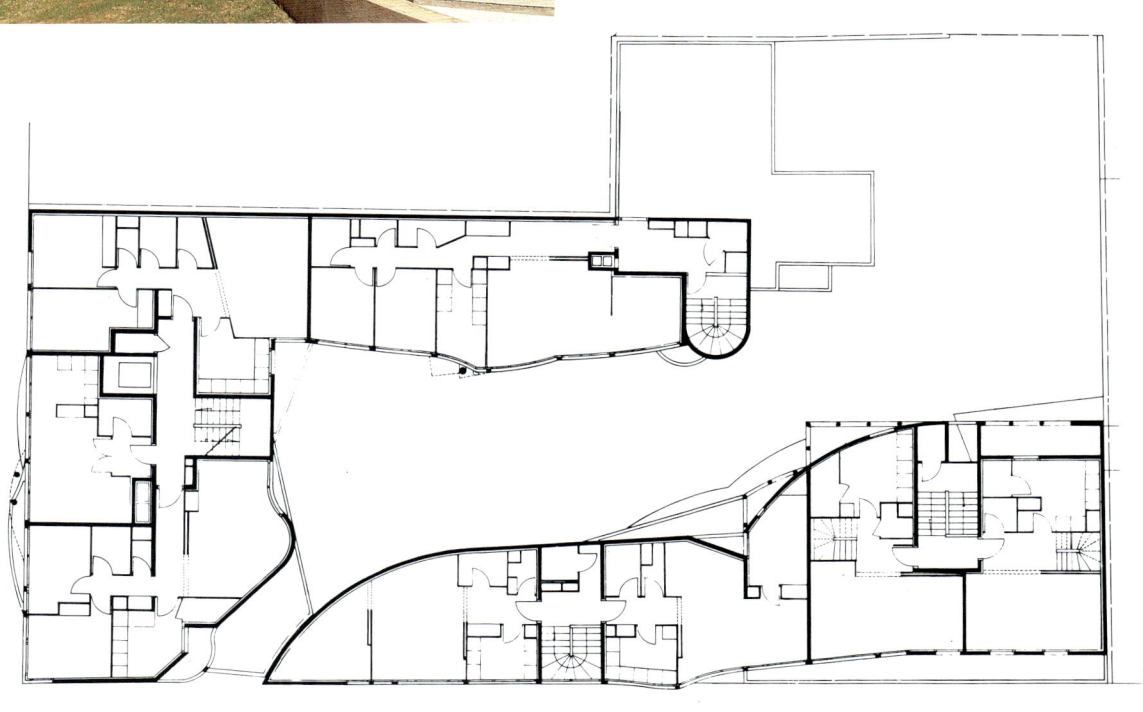

Haarlemmer Houttuinen Housing | Amsterdam, The Netherlands | 1978-1982

Herman Hertzberger

The Haarlemmer Houttuinen Housing in Amsterdam is squeezed between a busy main road and railway to the north and Haarlemmerstraat to the south. The north block was built by **Hertzberger**, the one to the south by the architects **Van Herk & Nagelkerke**. The two blocks are separated by a pedestrian street connected to Haarlemmerstraat by two gateway buildings also designed by **Van Herk**.

Hertzberger's housing block has projecting piers with balconies that give rhythm to the street. Each pier marks the entrance to four maisonettes and supports the balcony of the upper two. All entrances to the dwellings are off the street and balconies and gardens overlook it. Fine-tuning of scale is achieved by tiles in the centre of the lintels and the granite pads supporting them, and by the different sized square windows which syncopate rhythms and let in light along the ceilings where window heads have been kept closed to give intimacy within.

Hertzberger wanted the new street to be a *lively community area.* The street is accessible only to residents' cars and delivery vehicles. With the street closed to general motorised traffic and measuring only 7 metres in width, an unusually narrow profile by modern standards, a situation is created reminiscent of the old city. Street furnishings such as lights, bicycle racks, low fencing and public benches are distributed in such a way that the passage of traffic is obstructed with only a few parked cars. Some trees are planted to form a centre halfway between the two street sections. The lower maisonettes can be entered from their tiny gardens in the street, while the upper units can be reached by external stairs to a shared landing at first floor level, where the front doors are. While the extended block on the north side of the street provides shelter from the busy main road and railway behind it, the south-side block is one storey lower to allow the sun to shine in the street. In this respect, the scheme reinstates the original function of the street as a place where local residents can meet. Streets which no longer serve exclusively as traffic thoroughfares are increasingly seen on the new housing estates and in urban renewal projects. The interests of pedestrians are being taken into consideration, and with the recognition of the *woonerf* as a street space in a residential area where pedestrians enjoy legal protection against traffic, they are slowly regaining their rightful ground.

1932 Born in Amsterdam, The Netherlands.
1958 Graduated from the Technical University of Delft, The Netherlands.
1958 Started an architectural office.
1958-1963 Editor of 'Forum'.
1965-1969 Teacher, Academy of Architecture, Amsterdam, The Netherlands.
1966-1967 Visiting Professor at M.I.T., Cambridge, U.S.A.
1968 Visiting Professor, Columbia University, New York, U.S.A.
1968 Amsterdam Architecture Award, The Netherlands.
1969-1971 Visiting Professor, Toronto University, Canada.
Since 1970 Professor, the Technical University of Delft, The Netherlands.
1970 Visiting Professor, M.I.T., Cambridge, U.S.A.
1974 Visiting Professor, Toronto University, Canada.
1974 Eternit Award and Fritz-Schumacher Award.
1977 Visiting Professor, M.I.T., Cambridge, U.S.A.
1978 Visiting Professor, Tulane University, New Orleans, U.S.A.
1979 Visiting Professor, Harvard University, U.S.A.
1980 Visiting Professor, M.I.T., Cambridge, U.S.A.
1981 Visiting Professor, the University of Pennsylvania, U.S.A.
1982-1986 Visiting Professor, University of Geneva, Switzerland.
1987 Visiting Professor various universities in the U.S.A.

Major works
1968-1972 Office building 'Centraal Beheer', Amersfoort. The Netherlands (in co-operation with Lucas & Niemeijer).
1973-1978 Music centre 'Vredenburg', Utrecht, The Netherlands.
1978-1982 'Haarlemmer Houttuinen' Housing, Amsterdam, The Netherlands.
1980-1983 'Apollo Schools', Amsterdam, The Netherlands.

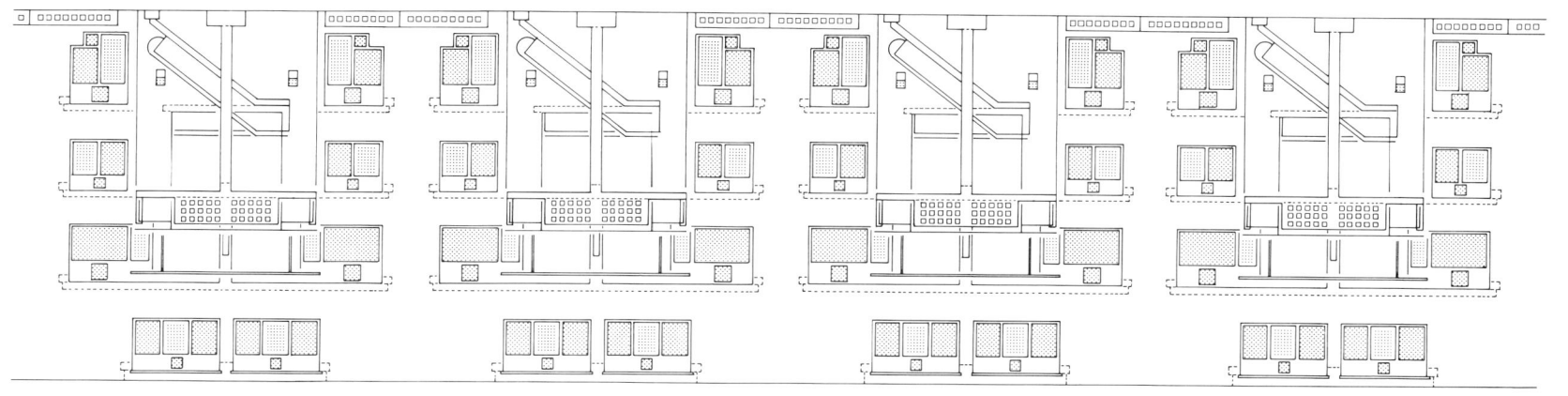

67

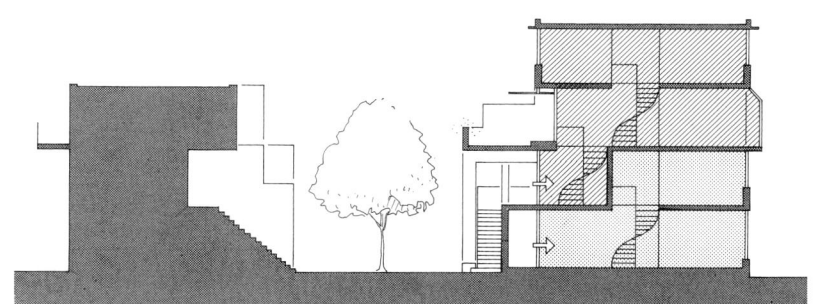

The decision to reserve a strip 27 metres wide flanking the railway for traffic purposes forced **Hertzberger** to build up to this imposed limit of alignment. As a result there was no room on this side for back gardens, which might in fact have been permanently in the shade. Unfavourable factors such as undesirable orientation and traffic noise meant that the north side would have to accommodate the rear wall, and so automatically all emphasis came to lie on the street side which faces south. The north side has no entrances or balconies. The long, continuous rear wall forms a sort of city wall marking the limits of the residential quarter and setting it apart from the railway viaduct, the open area beyond and the harbour in the distance. In order to involve the rear view in the architecture, the upper-storey dwellings were given bay windows. These are the only plastic features in an otherwise unarticulated wall.

Haarlemmer Houttuinen Housing | Herman Hertzberger

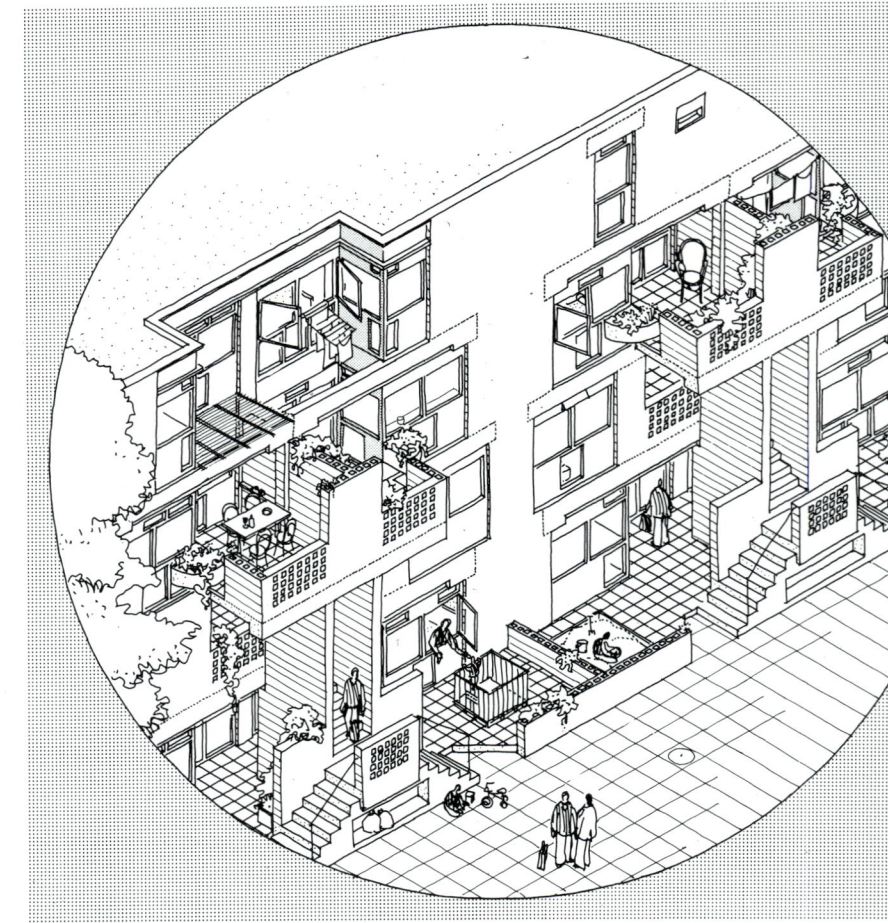

City Hall and Opera House | Amsterdam, The Netherlands | 1982-1988

Wilhelm Holzbauer

The City Hall and Opera House are located in the centre of Amsterdam in the area between Waterlooplein and the river Amstel. This area was once the centre of the old traditional Jewish quarter. After most of the Jewish population had been deported and many buildings destroyed during the last war, the area decayed.

The Opera House and City Hall complex offered an opportunity to revitalise this urban area. The decision to combine an Opera House and a City Hall in one urban complex may at first seem to be an arbitrary one. Indeed, in terms of function and contextual relations with the city they have little in common. However, **Wilhelm Holzbauer's** main object was to reanimate this area by attracting urban activity, and the functions of a City Hall would have been inadequate on their own.

Indirectly the building complex is the result of an international two-stage competition for a new City Hall, held in 1967/68. **Holzbauer's** entry won first prize and he was contracted to proceed with his plans. Changing politics and financial problems led to postponement and finally abandonment of the project. In a parallel development, plans for an Opera House in a residential area outside the city centre were also shelved. Until the new City Hall and Opera House complex was opened, Amsterdam had been the only Capital City in Europe without an opera. The idea of combining the Opera House and the City Hall in one complex on the central site originally reserved for the City Hall alone, was launched in 1979.

The architectural composition attempts to retain the distinctive expression of the two major functions within the ensemble. The individual parts of the building – the main auditorium and foyers, production and management areas for the Opera House on one hand, and the administrative areas and the main assembly hall of the City Hall on the other – all display their relationship with one of the two main functions.

The *flat surface* of the facade on the rectilinear, open space of Waterlooplein on the north side of the building contrasts sharply with the *plasticity* of the volumes along the river, where the semicircular form of the foyer responds to the bend that the river makes at this point.

The principle of breaking up the building programme into separate volumes and of rearranging these to form an architectural composition which ex-

1930 Born in Salzburg, Austria.
1945-1949 Studied at the Salzburg Technical College, Austria.
1950-1953 Studied at the Academy of Fine Arts, Vienna, Austria.
1952 Gold 'Füger' Medal.
1952-1956 Partnership with F. Kurrent and J. Spalt in Arbeitsgruppe 4.
1953 Austrian State Prize.
1954 Dr. Theodor Körner Prize
1956-1957 Studied at M.I.T., Cambridge, U.S.A.
1957-1958 Visiting Critic, University of Manitoba, Winnipeg, Canada.
1958-1959 Visiting Critic, Yale University, New Haven, U.S.A.
1959 Austrian State Prize.
1964 Started an architectural office in Vienna, Austria.
1967-1968 Guest seminars at the University of Illinois, Chicago, U.S.A.
1969 Started an architectural office in Amsterdam, The Netherlands.
1972 City of Vienna Prize, Austria.
1974 Guest Professor, Technical University of Graz, Austria.
1977 Full Professor, Academy of Applied Arts, Vienna, Austria.
1978 Awarded the Gold Medal of Honour by the City of Vienna, Austria.
1983 Reynolds Memorial Award.
1986 Salzburg Prize for Architecture, Austria.
1986 Landshauptstadt Salz-

burg Ring, Austria.
Since 1987 Dean of the Academy of Applied Arts, Vienna, Austria.

Honorary Fellow of the American Institute of Architects (A.I.A.).

Major works
Since 1971 Stations of the Vienna subway system, Austria.
1982-1988 City Hall and Opera House, Amsterdam, The Netherlands.
1982-1984 'IBA' municipal housing, Kreuzberg, Berlin, West Germany.
1982-1986 'ALRT' stations, Vancouver, Canada.

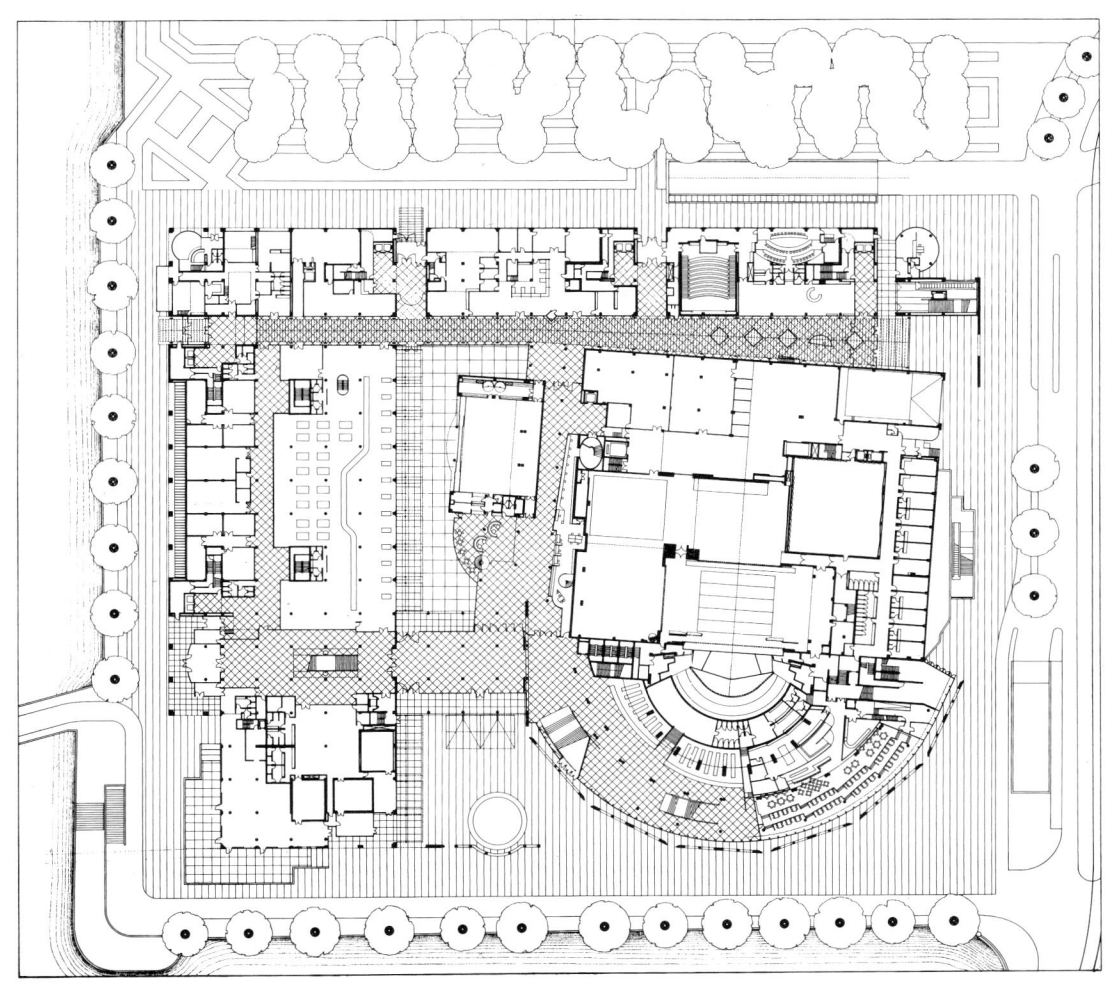

presses the two main functions of the building finds its correlation in the pattern of accessibility and the street patterns within the building.

The spatial and functional fusion of City Hall and Opera House takes place primarily at street level. The historical street pattern has been re-interpreted within the complex in the form of glass-covered passages, street-like spaces and inner courtyards. Entries are on all sides of the building. Their relative importance to either City Hall or Opera House is clearly expressed.

The formal dialogue between the two buildings and the differentiation of the architectural elements also find expression in the use of materials such as masonry, glass and marble, which express the hierarchy of functions within the building.

City Hall and Opera House | Wilhelm Holzbauer

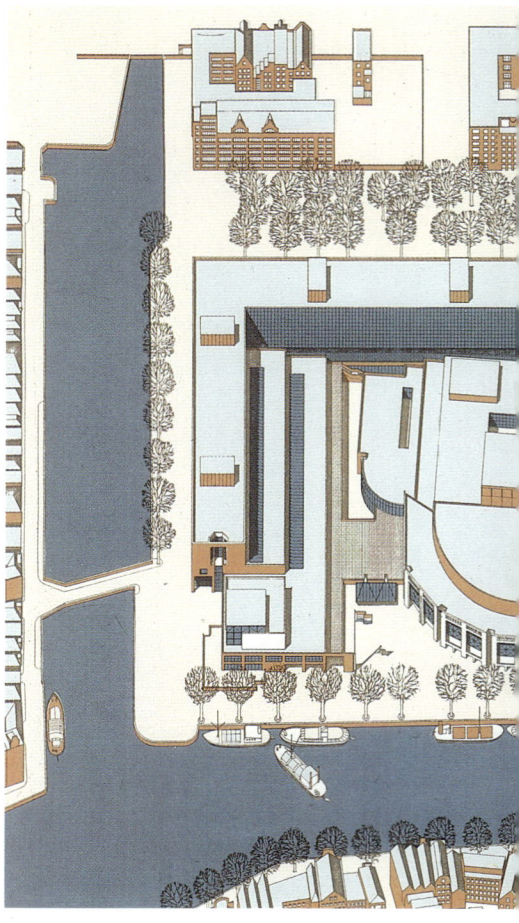

Creueta del Coll Park | Barcelona, Spain | 1987

Josep Martorell, Oriol Bohigas

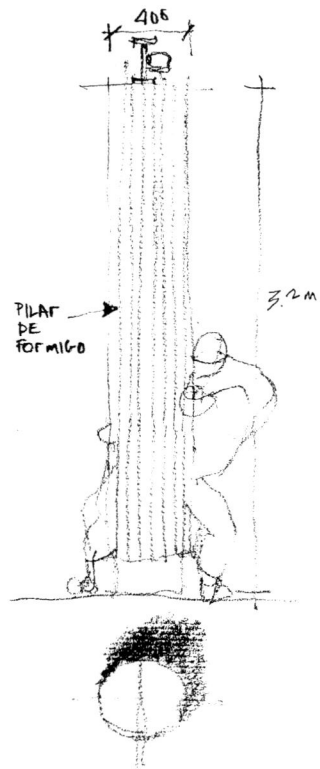

The site of this project is a partially quarried hillside with a surface of 16.41 hectares (40.55 acres), in a densely built-up area. The stone quarry had been abandoned, leaving the empty crater. There had been some illegal building on other parts of the hill, basically where these touched on bordering streets.

The park is divided into two sections, each with its own character. The north slope, looking towards Tibidabo mountain, was wasteland and treated as a reforestation area and provided with paths necessary to the laying out of play areas, clearings with picnic facilities, and an open-air theatre. Taking advantage of the structure of the edge of one part of the hillside, terraces were planned to accommodate a variety of sports facilities and link up with an open square, 1500 square metres in area, serving the residents of the adjoining neighbourhood of La Teixonera. On the south slope of the hill the main access steps to the park lead up from the Passeig Mare de Deu del Coll to a semicircular clearing of 6000 square metres set back against the walls of the quarry crater. Here we find two lakes, a plaza and some terraces. The main lake is 100 metres long and is suitable for swimming and boating. To one side, on a higher level, is another lake over which winds a boardwalk. The lakes are connected to each other by means of a waterfall. A small peninsula in the main lake is planted with palm trees. Instead of lawns there is a strip of paving for sunbathing. Beyond this paving is a semicircular plaza with play areas and a small planted area all edged by a curved row of trees and a paved walkway. A pergola constructed of concrete pillars follows the rim of the quarry, offering the opportunity to contemplate the entire spectacle for all of its 600-metre course. A small circular building for the sale of refreshments is placed at one end of this gangway.

The lake marks the transition from the semicircular clearing and the esplanade to the series of steps and terraces which make their way up to the rim of the crater in amphitheatre fashion. The terraces can accommodate large audiences for spectacles and concerts performed on the plaza. A system of paths with gentle gradients gives access to the different levels.

The paths and views of the park are given added interest by two large sculptures. At the end of the path coming in from the entrance is a vertical piece by artist **Ellsworth Kelly**. A large concrete sculpture by the Basque

1925 Born in Barcelona, Spain.
1951 Graduated from the School of Architecture, Barcelona, Spain.
1951 Partnership with Oriol Bohigas.
Since 1951 Founder member of Grup R.
1951-1956 Worked at the Office of the Provincial Town Planning Committee, Barcelona, Spain.
1961 Technical Diploma in Town Planning.
Since 1962 Partnership with David Mackay.
1963 Doctor in Architecture at the School of Architecture, Barcelona, Spain.
1968 President of the Cultural Committee of the College of Architects of Catalunya, Spain.
1970 Ministry Representative on the Town Planning Committee for the Metropolitan Area of Barcelona, Spain.
1979 Member of the Provincial Town Planning Committee, Barcelona, Spain.
1987 Director of Town Planning and Architecture of 'Villa Olimpica S.A.', Barcelona, Spain.
1988 Guest lecturer, seminar 'Urban Regeneration and the Shaping of Growth', Harvard Graduate School of Design and the Arab World Institute.

1925 Born in Barcelona, Spain.
1951 Graduated from the School of Architecture, Barcelona, Spain.
Since 1951 Partnership with Josep Martorell.
1951 Founder Member of Grup R.
1961 Technical Diploma in Town Planning, Barcelona, Spain.
Since 1962 Partnership with David Mackay.
1963 Doctor in Architecture at the School of Architecture, Barcelona, Spain.
1964-1966 Senior Lecturer, School of Architecture, Barcelona, Spain.
Since 1971 Chair in Composition, School of Architecture, Barcelona, Spain.
1974 Member of the Board of Directors of 'Arquitecturas bis', Barcelona, Spain.
1975 Member of the Board of Directors of 'Lotus International', Milan, Italy.
1976 Professor, Ball State University, Indiana, U.S.A.
1977-1980 Principal of the School of Architecture, Barcelona, Spain.
1980-1984 Director of City Planning, Barcelona, Spain.
1986 Gold Medal for Artistic Merit, Barcelona, Spain.
1988 Awarded the Medal of City Planning by the 'Fondation Académie d'Architecture de Paris', France.
1989 Sikkens Award, Rotterdam, The Netherlands.

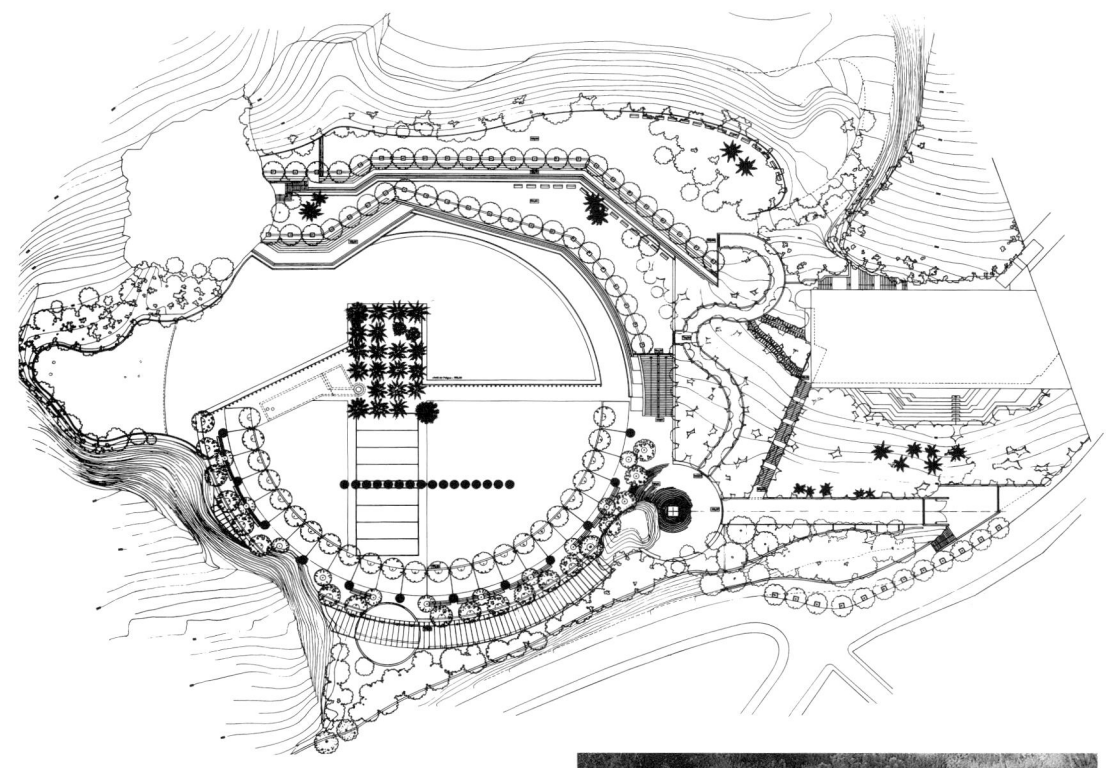

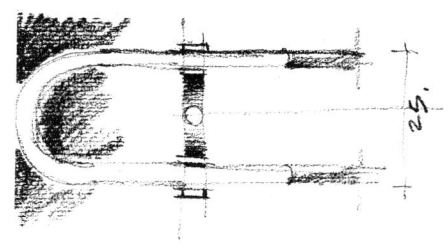

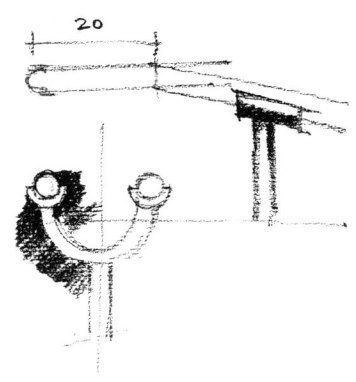

sculptor **Eduardo Chillida** hangs above the raised lake, suspended from four cables fixed directly into the rock.

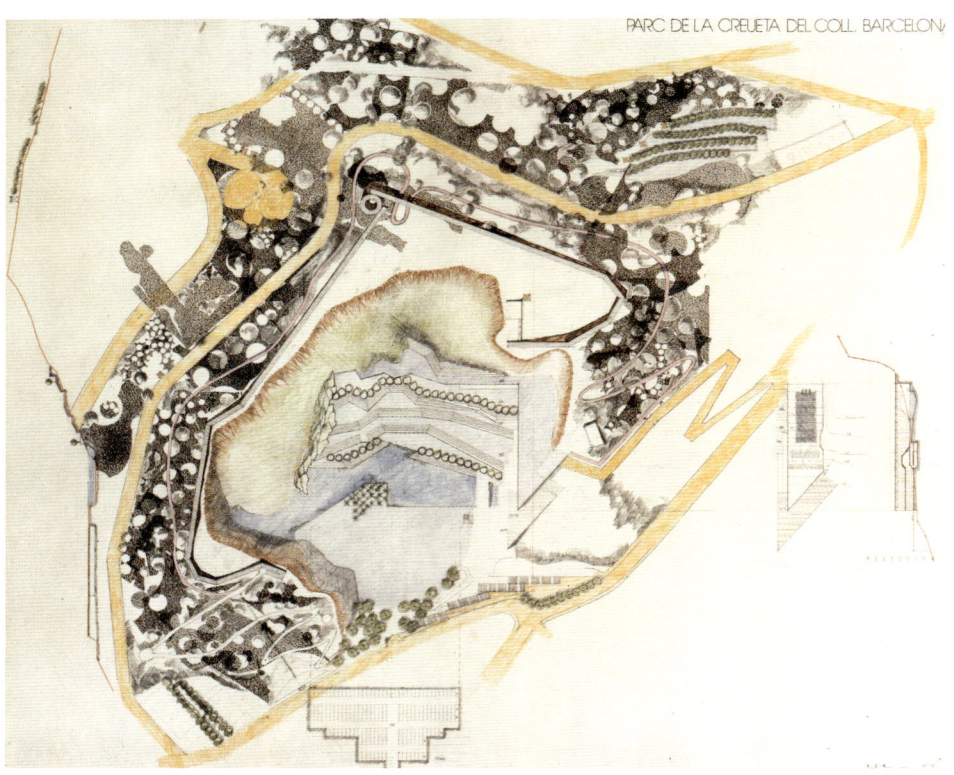

PARC DE LA CREUETA DEL COLL. BARCELONA

David Mackay

1933 Born in Eastbourne, Sussex, England.
1951 Part-time student at the Architectural Department at the Northern Polytechnic, London, England.
1956 State Scholarship for architectural studies.
1958 Honours Diploma in Architecture at the Northern Polytechnic, London, England.
1959 Settled in Barcelona.
1960 R.I.B.A. Andrew Prentice Burcer Prize for the study of Spanish architecture.
Since 1962 Partnership with Josep Martorell and Oriol Bohigas.
1966 Graduated from the School of Architecture, Barcelona, Spain.
1981 Professor, Washington University, St. Louis, U.S.A.
1985-1987 Professor of the post-graduate course in Landscape Design, School of Architecture, Barcelona, Spain.
1986 Distinguished Guest Professor, School of Architecture of Wisconsin University, Milwaukee, U.S.A.

Major works by Martorell, Bohigas and Mackay
1978-1980 Bank and Office building, Rambla de Mataró, Barcelona, Spain.
1983 Primary school, Sant Adrià del Besòs, Barcelona, Spain.
1987 The Creueta del Coll Park, Barcelona, Spain.
1987 Nestlé Office building Complex, Barcelona, Spain.

Creueta del Coll Park | Josep Martorell, Oriol Bohigas, David Mackay

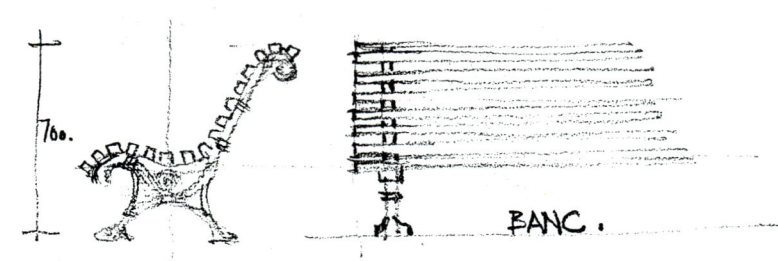

BANC.

National Museum of Roman Art | Mérida, Spain | 1980-1986

Rafael Moneo

Mérida, a town in the south-west of Spain, was founded in 25 B.C. by the Emperor **Augustus** at the crossing of the major roads between Salamanca and Sevilla, Toledo and Lisbon. It became the capital of Lusitania and was richly provided with monuments, of which a great many still stand. **Moneo** built his National Museum of Roman Art adjacent to an amphitheatre and a theatre, erected by Agrippa in 24 B.C., and over the archeological remains of a small Paleo-Christian basilica, a Roman house, an aqueduct and a road. He wanted the former grandeur to be reflected in the dimensions, volumes and richness of the new spaces, and built to a similar scale and using the same materials and methods as the Romans. The brick is used as permanent shuttering to massive unreinforced concrete walls with openings spanned by arches.

The new museum is a complex of three wings: the entry and administrative block, which contains a lecture room and a library on the upper levels; a large gallery block and a small workshop wing for bronze, mosaic and paper conservation.

The main entrance is from the top of the sloping Calle José Ramón Melida into the south elevation of the administration block at first floor level. The panelled entry doors at this side are surmounted by a niche with an antique statue. Inside, the administration block is organised around a well that opens up from the entry level to the roof, drawing attention to the lecture theatre and library above. From the entrance hall a ramp leads down to the main museum level on the ground floor. Here a bridge across the sunken court leads to the nave of the museum. Following the ramp down, the landing at the half level connects to a tunnel that leads under the Calle José Ramón Melida to the amphitheatre and theatre, which may be visited with the same ticket. At the bottom of the ramp is a triangular hall closed across its hypotenuse by the remaining aqueduct of San Lazaro. From here is access to the sunken court and the cafeteria that opens out onto it. Beyond the Roman road are the steps down to the excavations below the museum. **Moneo** aimed to *intertwine the ruins and the new construction in such a way that visitors would feel that the ruins led an independent existence beyond the confines of the building.* Instead of incorporating the ruins as an isolated fragment in the museum, he allowed rows of arches to cut through

1937 Born in Tudela, Spain.
1958-1961 Worked in the office of F.J. Saenz de Oiza.
1961 Graduated from the Madrid School of Architecture, Spain.
1961-1962 Worked in the office of Jörn Utzon, Denmark.
1963-1965 Fellow of the Spanish Academy, Rome, Italy.
1965 Started an architectural office in Madrid, Spain.
1966-1970 Assistant Professor, School of Architecture, Madrid, Spain.
1971-1985 Professor of Architecture, School of Architecture, Barcelona, Spain.
Since 1974 Member of the editorial board of 'Arquitecturas Bis'.
1976-1977 Visiting Fellow of the Institute for Architectural and Urban Studies, New York, U.S.A.
1976-1977 Visiting Professor, Cooper Union School for Architecture, New York, U.S.A.
1980 Professor, School of Architecture, Madrid, Spain.
Since 1985 Chairman of the Graduate School of Design, Harvard University, Cambridge, U.S.A.

Major works
1971-1974 Housing block with picture gallery, Madrid, Spain.
1976-1981 City Hall, Logroño, Spain.
1980-1986 National Museum of Roman Art, Mérida, Spain.

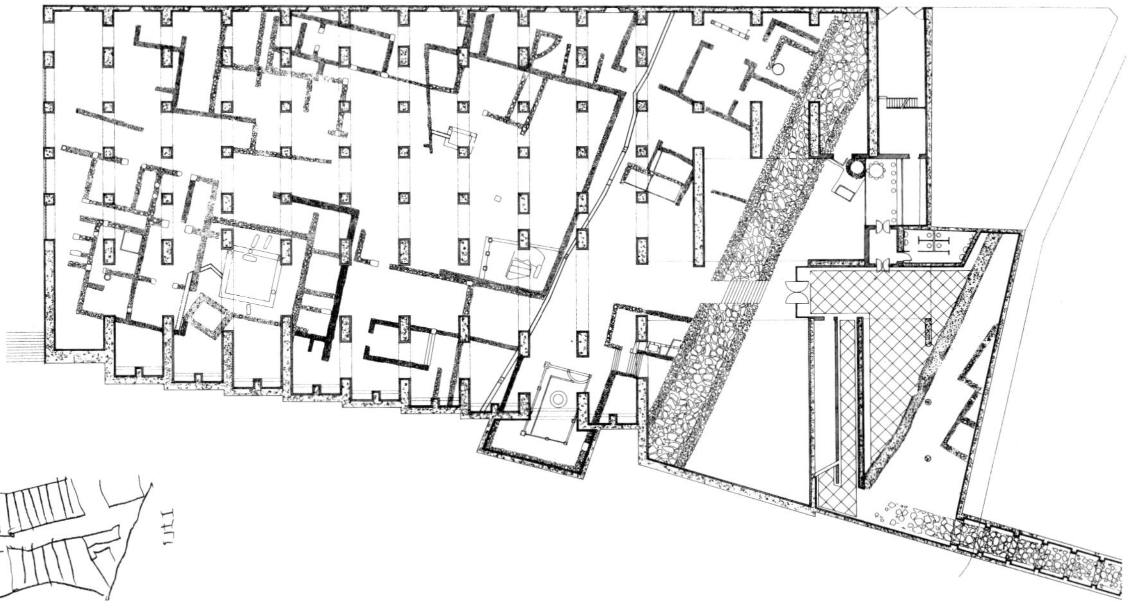

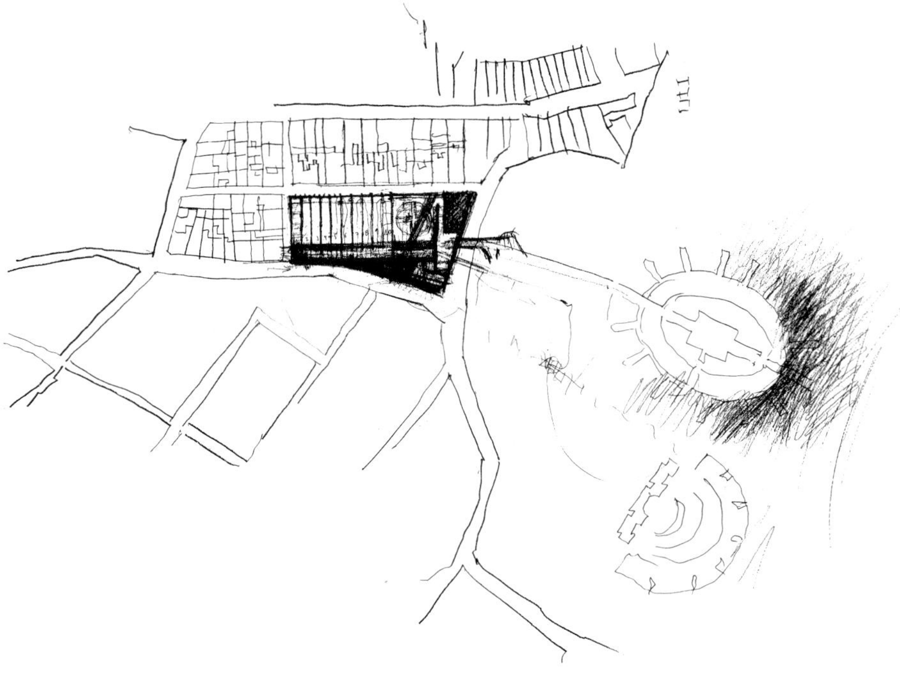

the excavations, breaking step into larger arches here and there to avoid key remains. Over all these he spread a continuous slab. The new structure in the underground level has its own orientation, different from that of the ruins. Though the excavations are under the museum and only accessible through it, they are experienced as if they were out of door. Light enters along the edges of this undercroft.

In contrast to the dark basement, the space in the museum is flooded with light that falls from above. The grand gallery wing, close to 50 feet high, is organised by lateral bearing walls spaced 20 feet apart. These walls, of concrete clad in brick, are interrupted by a variety of arched openings. To the north of the central nave are two mezzanine levels. Individual galleries on these mezzanines are separated by the lateral walls, connected horizontally by arched openings and vertically by openings in the floor. Stairs between the gallery levels occur at both sides of the wing. The flat, reinforced concrete slabs of the mezzanine levels are thin and modern, as are the steel railings, in order to contrast with the ancient look of the thick arched brick-faced walls.

National Museum of Roman Art | Rafael Moneo

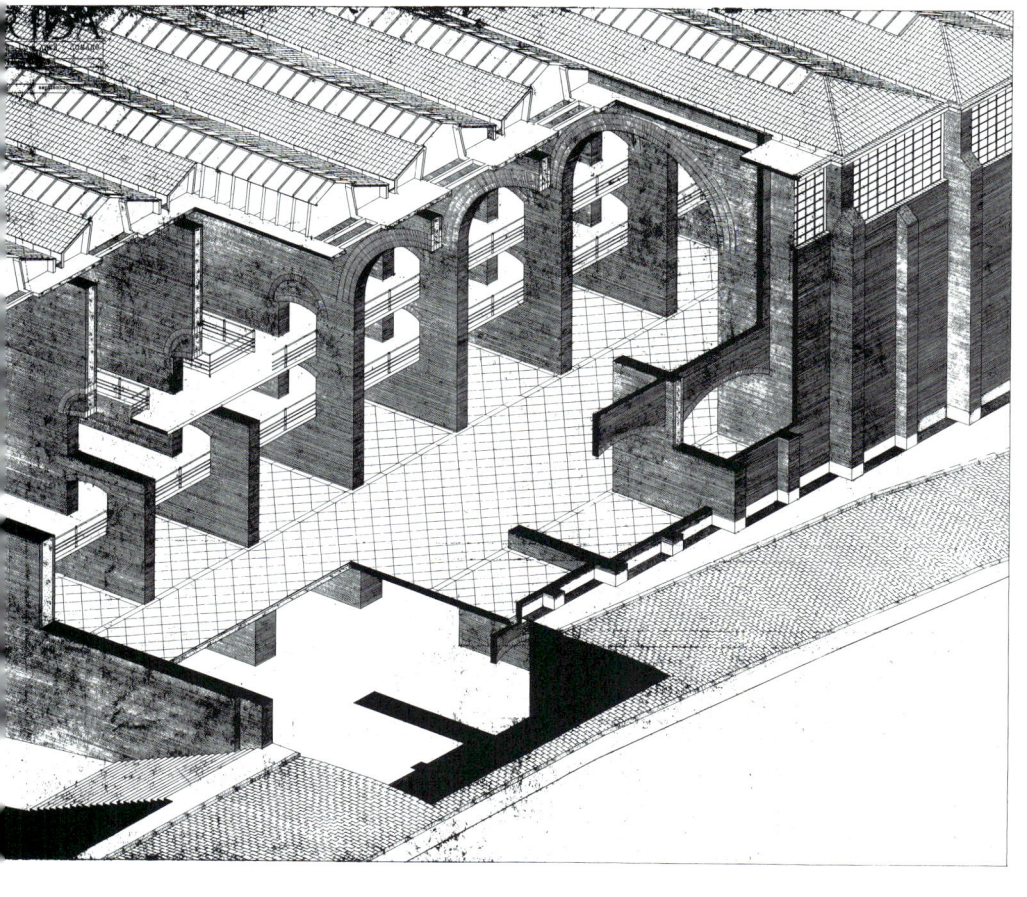

The bank, the headquarters of the Casa Rurale e Artigiana, is situated on the outskirts of the small town of Alzate Brianza in the north of Italy. The area is no longer rural but not yet fully urban. It is a narrow, deep site (50 × 150 metres) surrounded by a random collection of houses, open space and small industrial buildings and set between a main road linking Como and Bergamo and a minor local road.

Natalini has responded to the problem of designing a large new public building for this suburban setting by emphasising the monumental qualities of the bank as a prominent urban building type. In this building *he has investigated the possibility of a meeting and hybridisation between past and present, between tradition and sophisticated construction techniques and between the classical and the vernacular.* The language of the building is up-to-date with simply and strongly marked forms, such as open-plan floors, a continuous facade and sun-break. At the same time, however, it evokes the techniques, language and architectural features of the Italian Romanesque period. This can be seen in the pilasters, pilaster strips and the stone facing.

The building has been planned as a long, narrow, rectangular block with two triangular prisms at its extremities. An undulating screen wall, a sort of unrolled cylinder, stands free of the regular structural frame and forms the entrance to the main public banking hall at one end of the building. Projecting from the front, and facing the minor road, is a block that contains the caretaker apartment. It is set at an angle to the main block. The building is placed diagonally across the site. This strategy frees space for vehicle access and parking, while orienting the building towards the distant town centre. It also makes it appear foreshortened from the road, increasing its plastic and dynamic effect.

The bank consists of three levels of clear space above ground. The two triangular prisms house all services. A hidden basement provides additional space for secure parking and service functions.

The load-bearing structure is completely external to the building. Apart from the obvious functional benefits of 12 metre-deep, column-free internal spaces which can be easily subdivided to suit the client's changing needs, this creates a monumental arcade along the sides of the building. The ar-

1941 Born in Pistoia, Italy.
1966 Graduated in Architecture from the University of Florence, Italy.
1966 Started 'Superstudio'.
1986 National 'Tercas' Prize for architecture.
1987 International Award for Architecture in Stone.
1988 Marble Architectural Award, Italy.
1989 Winner of the National Competition for Design in Granite.
1989 Resident Professor, School of Architecture, University of Florence, Italy.

Member of the Association of German Architects (B.D.A.)

Major works
1983-1984 Bank, Alzate Brianza, Italy.
1984 House Römerberg, Frankfurt, West Germany.
1984-1987 Teatro della Compagnia, Florence, Italy.

Adolfo Natalini

82

Bank | Alzate Brianza, Italy | 1983-1984

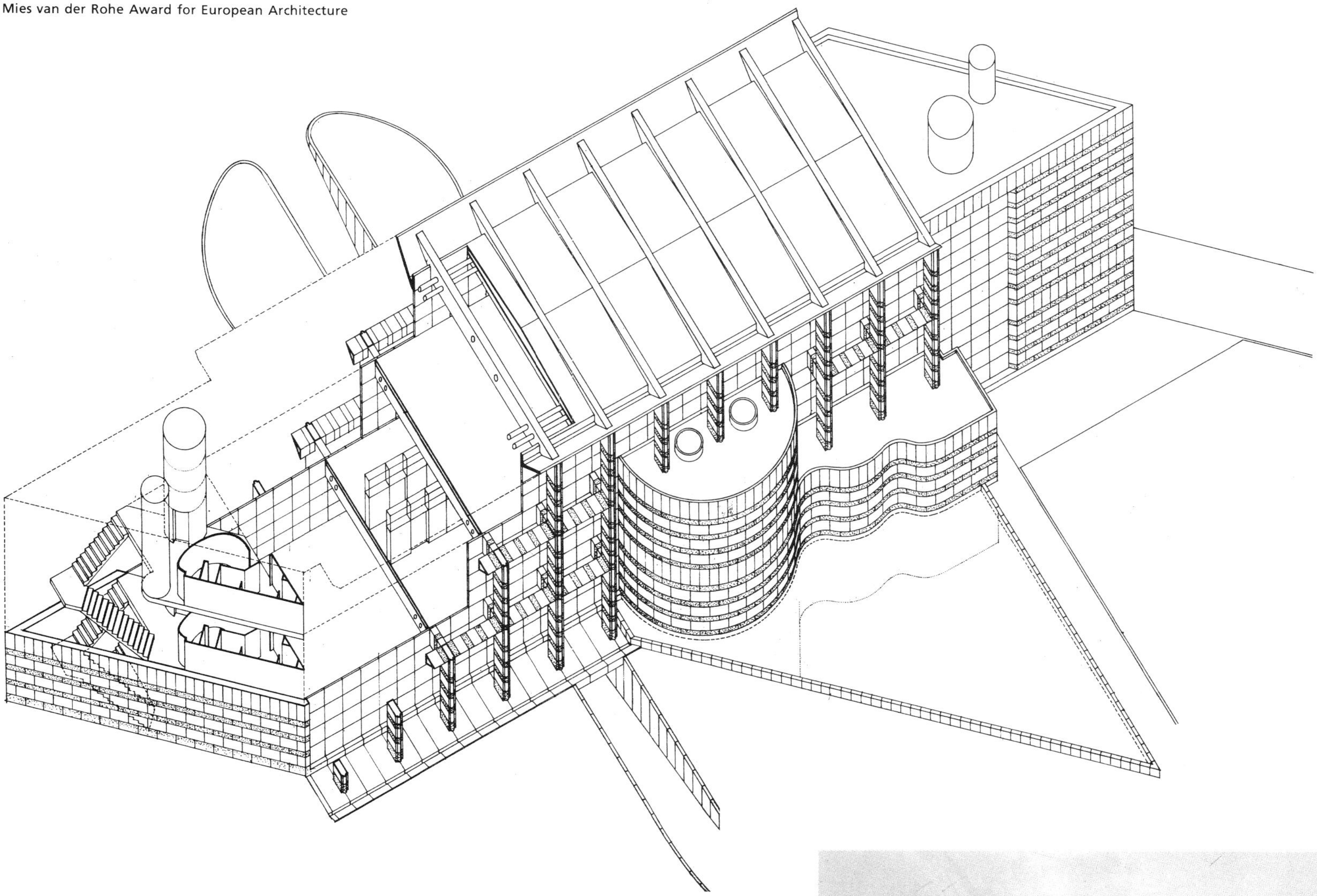

cade is used to screen the walls of the offices behind. Shaded by the structure, the unbroken facades are completely faced with glass in slender frames of black neoprene.

To contrast the heavy structure with the light glassy spaces within, the whole of the arcade is clad in stone. This cladding is striped in dark and light grey bands of polished siliceous and light-shot granite to achieve a striking dichromatism which is emphasised by alternating shiny and opaque surface treatments. The arcade's stone cladding is delicately modelled with half-rounded pilasters. The same facing is applied to the triangular prisms housing the services and the undulating block that projects from the structure. The whole of the facing is detached from the walls and the structure to accomodate ventilated wall technique. Seven millimetre-wide gaps between the stones are left open for ventilation.

Inside the building public spaces are at ground floor level. They are within largely open spaces which are finished throughout in stone. The offices above, which have a wide range of functions, are fitted within a glazed box by using a conventional but thoughtfully selected kit consisting of elegant standardised partitioning systems, integrated suspended ceilings and carpeted floors, all planned on a 1-2 metre grid. Within the triangular prisms the stairs are exposed, while the lifts and service risers are enclosed by curving and colourful mosaic-faced walls.

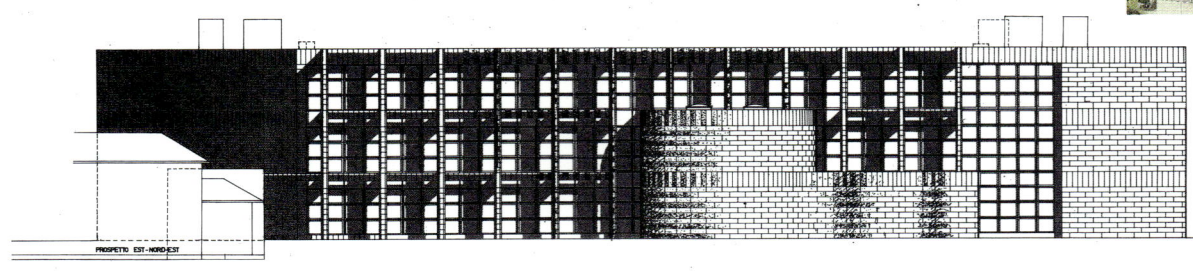

Bank | Adolfo Natalini

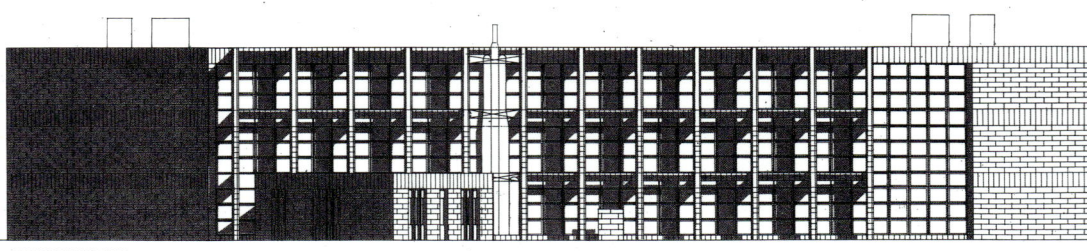

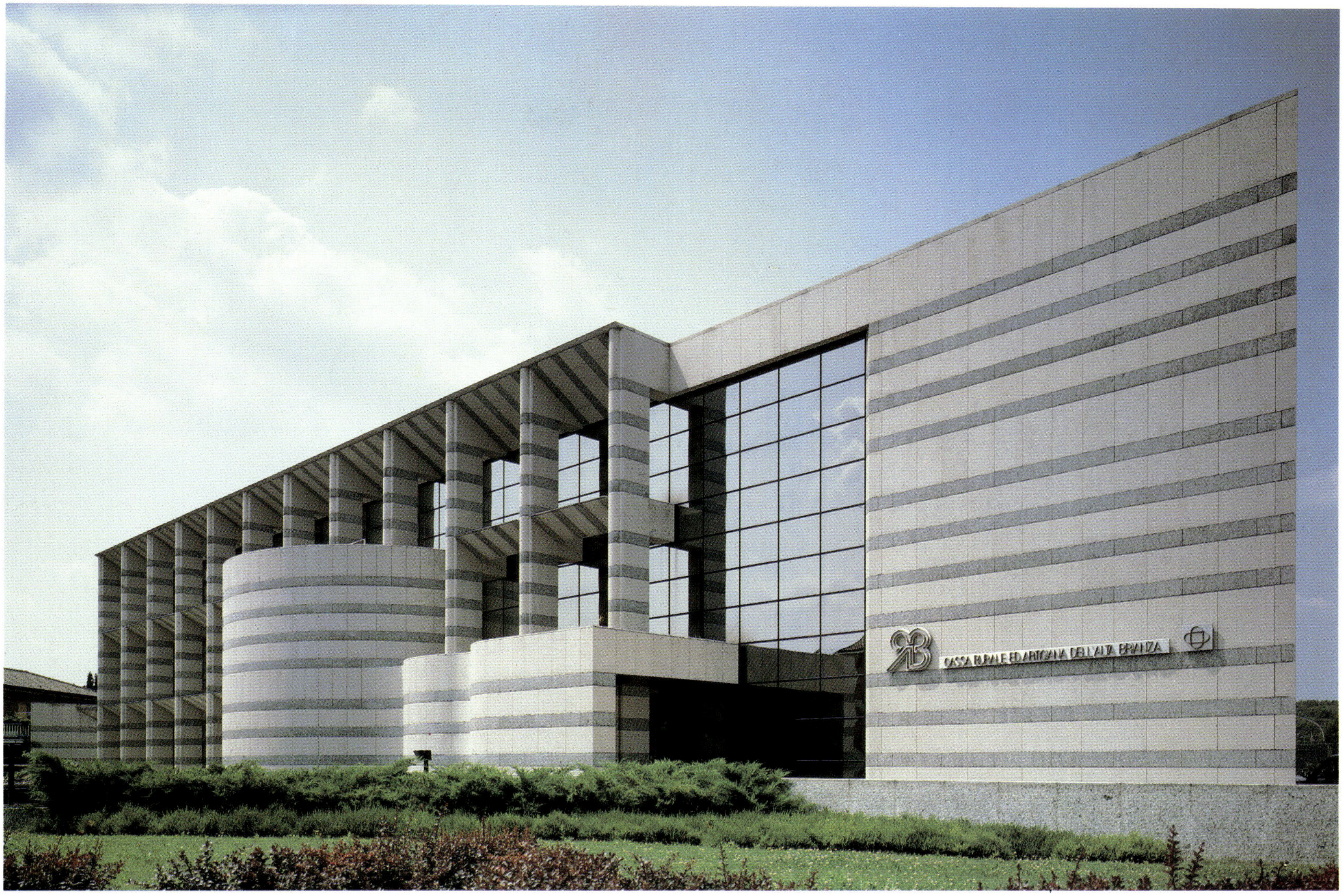
CASSA RURALE ED ARTIGIANA DELL'ALTA BRIANZA

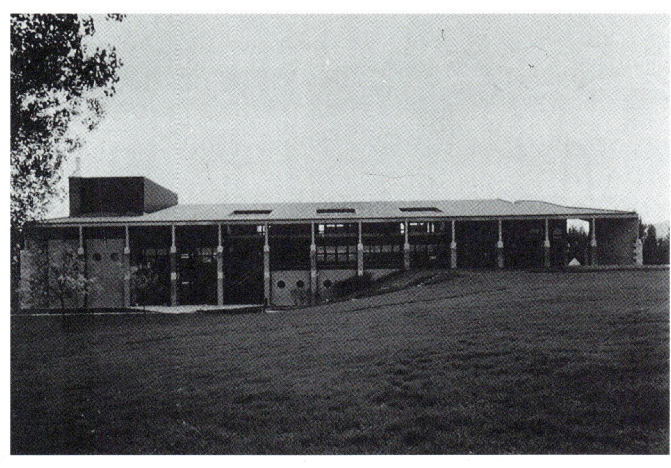

Arab Cultural Centre | Paris, France | 1987

Jean Nouvel

The Arab Cultural Centre in Paris is located at the very end of the Boulevard St. Germain, on the corner of Quai St. Bernard and Rue des Fosses, on the Left Bank of the river Seine, facing Ile St. Louis.

Originally a site near the Eiffel Tower was chosen for the Institute's building, but after the Socialist government was elected in 1981, these plans were abandoned and the architectural aspects of the project radically reconsidered. Now the building is situated on the boundary of the old centre of Paris and the modern city and functions as a bridge between them.

The purpose of the Institute was to increase knowledge of the Arab world, its language, cultural and spiritual values; to promote exchange and co-operation between France and the Arab countries, particularly in the fields of science and industry; and to enhance relations between the Arab world and Europe.

A limited architectural competition was won by **Jean Nouvel** with his associates **Pierre Soria**, **Gilbert Lézènes** and **Architecture Studio**. The design concept of the Institute has remained unchanged from the winning competition scheme.

The Institute's premises include a museum, a library, an audiovisual room, a council chamber, an auditorium, several staff offices, a restaurant and canteen and a car park. The design addresses three principal dichotomies: the traditional and modern aspects of the site; Arab and Western cultures; and interiority and openness. For **Nouvel**, none of this implies literal-minded mimicry of Arab or Parisian forms, but an opportunity to *pursue his own preoccupations with stratification, surface tension and diffraction to create an architectural form and image of the present.*

The form of the building came from an analysis of the site and its central Paris context. The great curve to the northern wing rounds off a notional line, projecting between Boulevard St. Germain and Quai St. Bernard. The southern facade of the building lines up with the existing university block next door and defines a rectilinear open space which, notionally at least, could be linked to the Jardin des Plantes. The slit between the northern and southern ranges is seen as a suitable response to the apse of the Notre Dame cathedral, while the *Tower of Books* at the building's western extremity is intended as a landmark, terminating the vistas at the end of Boulevard

1945 Born in Fumel, France.
1971 Graduated from E.N.S.B.A.
1976 Co-founder of the 'Mars 1976' movement.
1979 Co-founder of the Syndicat de l'Architecture.
1987 'Grand Prix d'Architecture'.
1987 Silver Square Award.

Chevalier de l'Ordre du Mérite.
Chevalier des Arts et Lettres.
Médaille d'Argent de l'Académie d'Architecture.

Major works
1974 School, Trelissac, France.
1983 Theatre, Belfort, France.
1987 Institute of the Arab World, Paris, France.
1987 Cultural Centre, Saint Herblain, France.

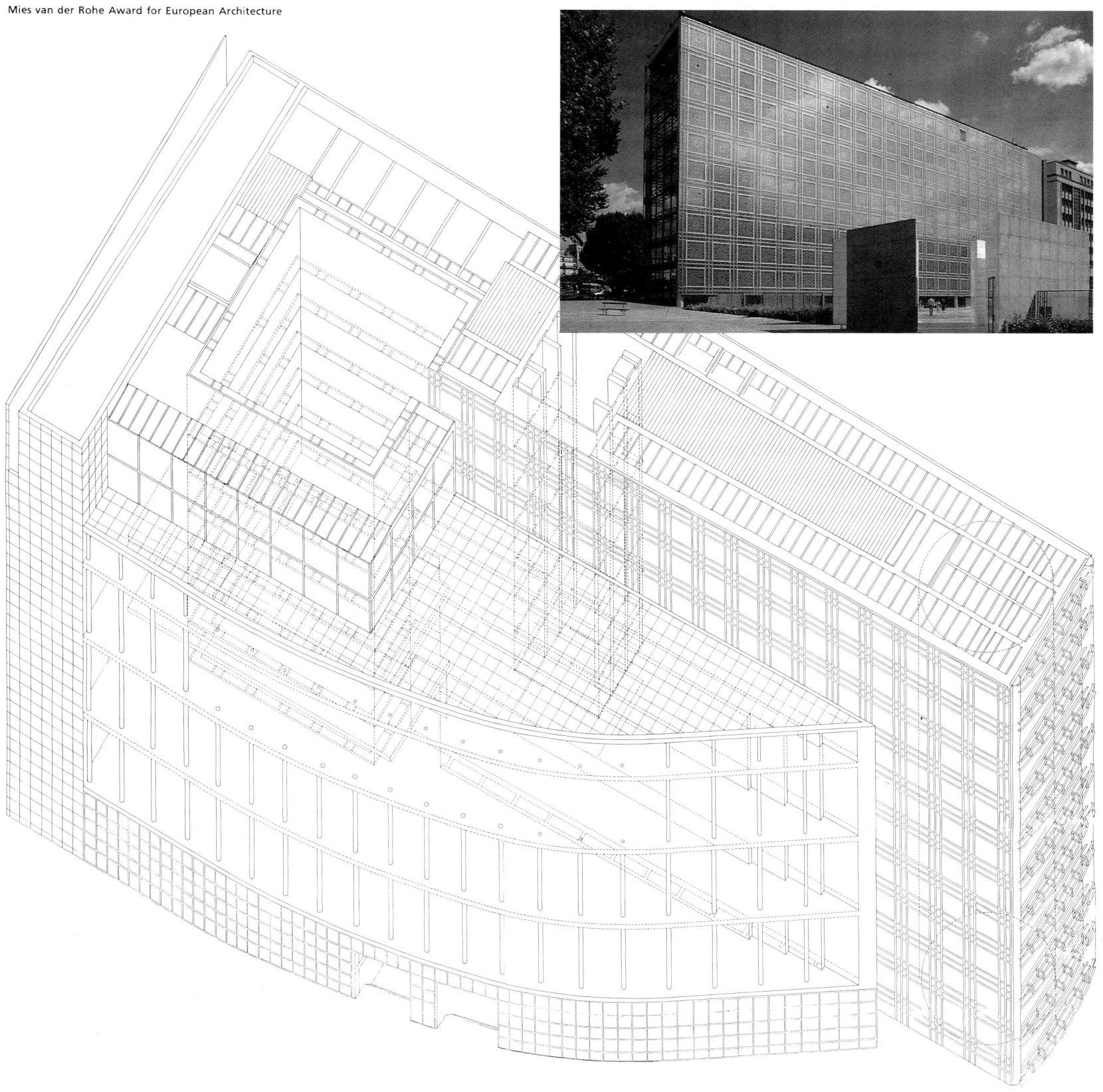

St. Germain, from Ile St. Louis and from the Sully bridge.

The architectural concept is based entirely on attractiveness to, and reception of, the public and on the notion of a showcase for Arab culture.

The most striking part of the building is the south-west wall with its *aluminium iris diaphragms* which respond electronically to the intensity of sunlight. It is a conscious technological interpretation of Islamic *mushrabiyyas,* the carved wooden screens found over external openings in Islamic buildings. The form of the diaphragms and the pattern of light and shade they create provide an immediate visual allusion to traditional Arab culture by modern Western means.

The central court is lined with squares of marble clamped in a simple, but decorative, metal frame, which form a translucent screen outside the glazing. The court contains a fountain of mercury, which recalls the interior of the palace in the story of 1001 Nights and mystifies the place.

The Arab Cultural Centre draws certain themes from Islamic architecture, but at the same time it is a French exploration of high technology.

Arab Cultural Centre | Jean Nouvel

The Phosphate Elimination Plant built by the Austrian architect **Gustav Peichl** is situated in Berlin's northern district of Tegel. The complex, a project of Internationale Bauausstellung (IBA), was built to ensure a continuing supply of drinking water for West Berlin from its own lakes, and to make the Tegeler Lake suitable for leisure activities. For town-planning reasons, the overall complex of the plant has been designed to contain as many green areas as possible. Three circular flocculation vats were covered with soil to create a triangular green embankment with an uninterrupted slope on all sides down to the grassed area. The dominant impression of the plant at ground level is of a great ship which has crashed into this embankment.

The project aimed to *integrate the technical and functional conception with the architectural design*. The external appearance is a product of the architectural solution and the technical and functional demands. The *radial* form of the geometric plan is based on technical and hydraulic requirements and is subsequently retained in the organisation of the buildings. The individual functional units (flocculation vats and their underlying filtration systems) are arranged radially at the centre of the plant in the shape of a star, giving rise to short and rectilinear conduits and passages. Even the main unit, the engine-room building, with its organisational spaces and operational equipment, is radially coordinated to the functional centre of the plant. This main building houses the functional system. It has an elongated shape and a curved facade concave to the centre. The heart of the installation, the control room with its observation platform, is located on the upper floor and resembles the bridge of a large ship.

The design of the building is determined by the differentiation of architectonic masses and by simple effects of the materials used. The outer walls are partly plastered, painted and tiled; the window frames are made of metal to save energy, and the roofing is of sheet metal, with an internal channel to carry off water.

The building is traversed vertically by a stairwell equipped with a combination of lifts and service elevators. The stairs and service elevator reach from the basement to the second floor. Access to the ground floor is possible from the north and the south side of the building. On the first and second floors, working areas are reached from central corridors. Provision is

1928 Born in Vienna, Austria.
1949-1953 Studied at the Academy of Fine Arts, Vienna, Austria.
1953 Started an architectural office in Vienna, Austria.
1969 City of Vienna Award for Architecture.
1971 Austrian State Award for Architecture.
1973 Professor, Academy of Fine Arts, Vienna, Austria.
1975 Reynolds Memorial Award, U.S.A.

Member of the 'Österreichischen Kunstsenats'.
Member of the Academy of Arts, Berlin, Germany.
Honorary member of the Association of German Architects (B.D.A.).
Honorary member of the Royal Institute of British Architects (R.I.B.A.).

Major works
1965-1967 Rehabilitation centre, Vienna, Austria.
1979-1981 Studios for the Austrian Broadcasting Company, Graz, Austria.
1979-1981 Studios for the Austrian Broadcasting Company, Eisenstadt, Austria.
1985 Phosphate elimination plant, Berlin, Germany.

Gustav Peichl

Phosphate Elimination Plant | Tegel-Berlin, West Germany | 1985

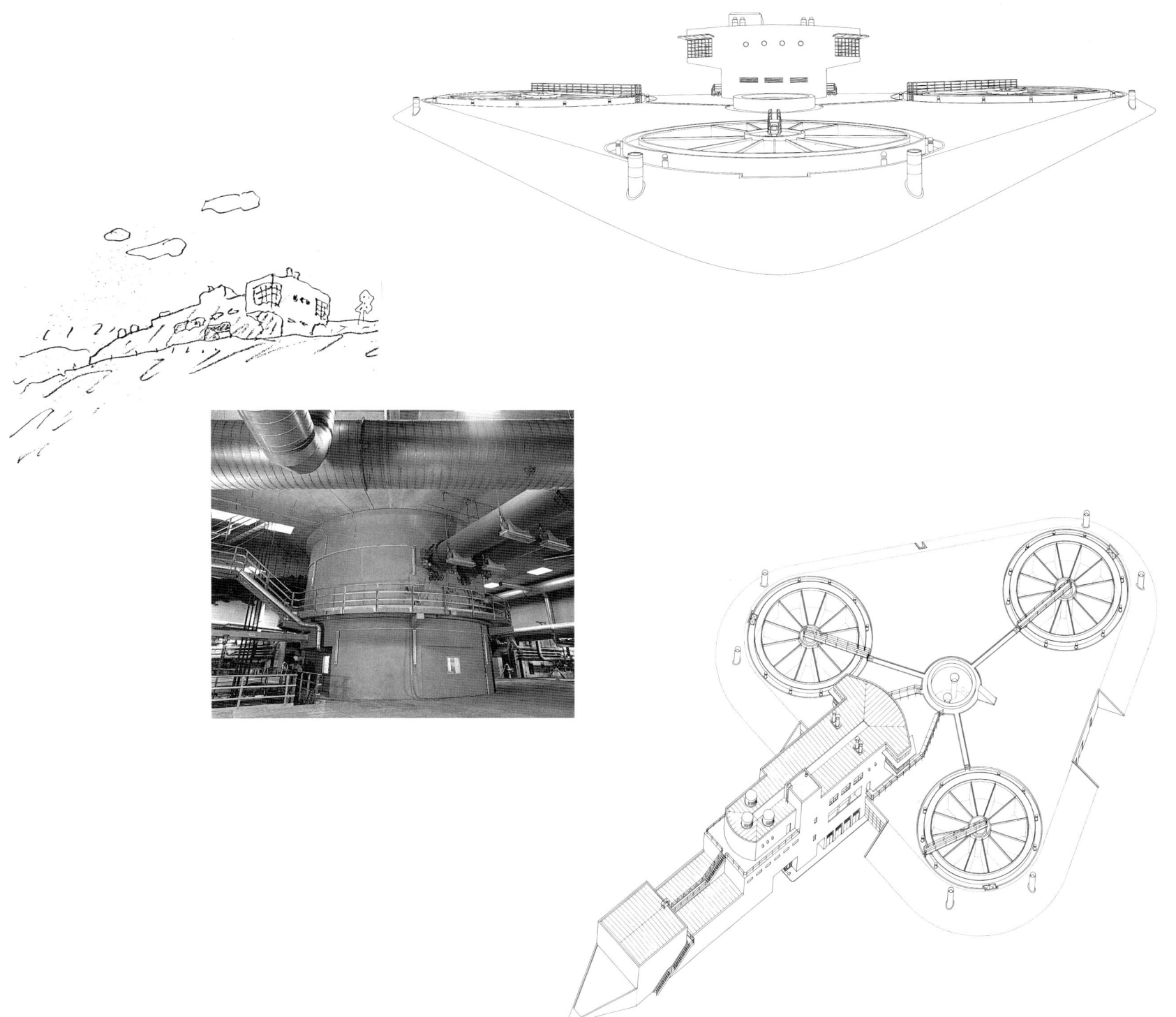

made on the first floor for exits onto the embankment surrounding the vats. From the meeting hall located on the second floor, another suspended staircase descends, first over the roof of the batching station, then laterally to the base level of the plant. The main staircase serves as the main entrance.

The batching station, storage for chemicals and the workshop are all directly accessible from the courtyard of the building. Access to the basement is via the stairwell, the lift or further flights of stairs, including an emergency one. The central zone of the building can be traversed at ground floor level by a connecting passage leading to the chlorine station and the pump room.

Phosphate Elimination Plant | Gustav Peichl

Schlumberger Factories | Montrouge-Paris, France | 1980-1985

The Montrouge site was acquired by Schlumberger in the 1970s as a functioning heavy industrial complex with 125,000 square metres of work space for 4500 employees. In the course of the decade, Schlumberger switched from heavy engineering to the production of precision equipment for the information industries, such as electronic detection methods in oil fields. As a result of this change, there was a need for facilities that could accommodate 2000 people engaged in office work, research and precision light-engineering.

Because the price of land in greater Paris had soared, the company was forced to give up the idea of buying a new site to build manufacturing facilities. Instead it was decided to renovate the existing group of buildings that stood in a regular arrangement on the large site, which is diagonally divided by the Avenue Jean Jaurès. The new accommodation was to be both simple and flexible, and capable of being adapted to changing needs, including possible sale or letting of separate plots. The phasing of the conversion had to allow for continuing use of part of the premises throughout the process, and the end product had to enhance the immediate neighbourhood.

Ideas were sought from over 20 architectural and industrial design practices, and finally the proposal put forward by **Renzo Piano** was adopted. He envisaged the least change to the buildings, and suggested *retaining the blocks at the perimeter of the site and clearing the centre to provide a staff car park.* His project had three main objectives: first, to maintain the outward appearance of the old factory, which had for so long been the mainstay of production; second, to rearrange the interior organisation of each of the structures, while changing parts of them and bringing them more into line with present requirements; third, to replace the single-storey factory building at the centre of the site by a large garden.

Almost all of the buildings retained were of concrete frame construction except for the top floors, which were steel-framed, with steel roof-trusses. The original infill panels were of clinker brick with horizontal bands of metal-framed casement windows. **Piano** used the original concrete frame as a grid into which he inserted new elements. He also retained a major part of the floors and external infill.

More or less in the middle of each block, there is an entrance zone. In the

Renzo Piano

1937 Born in Genoa, Italy.
1964 Graduated from the School of Architecture, Milan Polytechnic, Italy.
1962-1964 Worked with Franco Albini.
1965-1970 Worked with Louis I. Kahn in Philadelphia and Z.S. Makowsky in London.
1971-1977 Partnership with Richard Rogers (Atelier Piano & Rogers).
1977 Partnership with Peter Rice (Atelier Piano & Rice).
1980 Partnership with Richard Fitzgerald in Houston, U.S.A.
1980 Partnership with Shunji Ishida in Genoa, Italy.
1981 Golden Compass.
1984 Commandeur dans l'Ordre des Arts et Lettres.
1985 Chevalier de la Légion d'Honneur.
1989 R.I.B.A. Gold Medal.

Visiting Professor at Columbia University, New York, U.S.A.; University of Pennsylvania, Philadelphia, U.S.A.; Oslo School of Architecture, Norway; Polytechnic of Central London, England; Architectural Association, London, England.
Honorary Fellow of the American Institute of Architects (A.I.A.).
Honorary Fellow of the Royal Institute of British Architects (R.I.B.A.).

Major works
1977 Georges Pompidou Centre, Paris, France (with Richard Rogers and Ove Arup).
1980-1985 The Schlumberger factories, Montrouge, Paris, France.
1981-1983 Menil Museum, Houston, U.S.A.
1987 Football stadium, Bari, Italy.

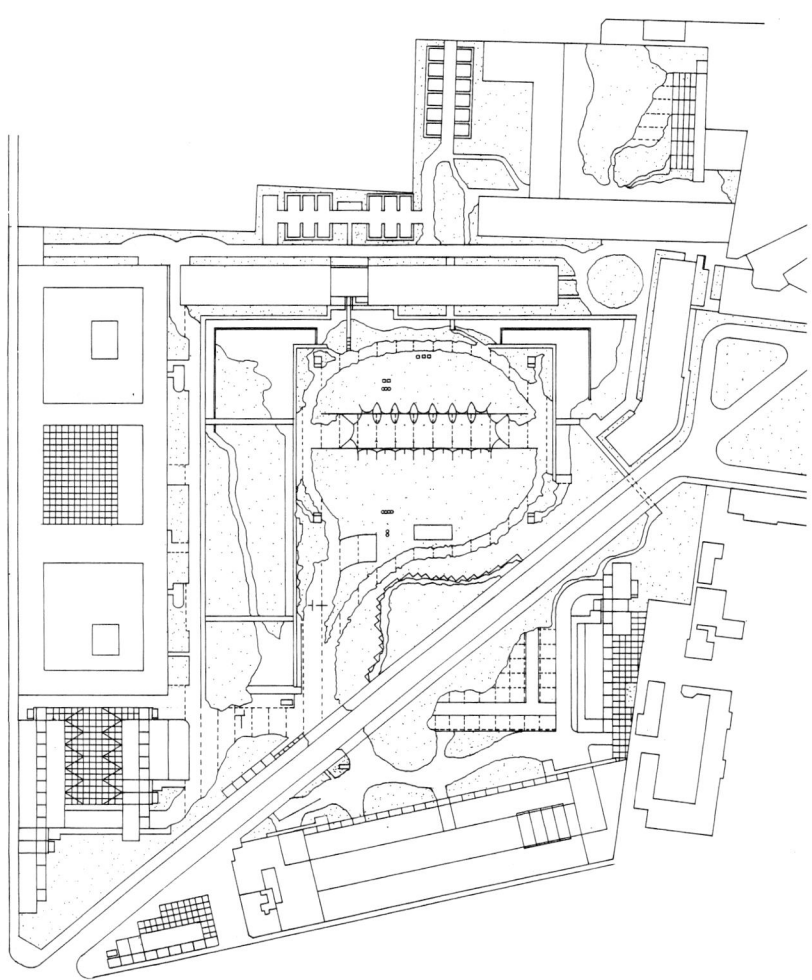

middle of the northern block, **Piano** removed the original infill panels to create a main entrance. A glazed skin is suspended beneath the original roof trusses and behind the concrete frame over the full height of the building, forming a greenhouse-type space into which steel staircases and lifts have been introduced.

Piano adopted a kit system for the steel staircases, the elevators, facades, facing panels and street furniture to tie together what was newly constructed and the existing structures. The kit elements were colour-coordinated: grey for the concrete structure, green for the window frames, red for the steel structure, blue for the air conditioning, and bright yellow for all the elements in the circulation areas.

The entrances to the blocks are linked to the central landscaped area by bridges. Beneath this central area is a parking area for 1000 cars and on top of it there is a facility known as the *'Forum'* which is shared by the various companies in the Schlumberger Group located around the site. The *Forum* is hidden by the contoured landscaping and Teflon tenting. It contains communal facilities such as a multipurpose hall for meetings, exhibitions, lectures and other functions, a restaurant, a bank and a travel agency. People thus come up from the underground car park, pass under the Teflon tenting and walk through the large landscaped garden, designed by **Alexandre Chemetoff,** to their place of work.

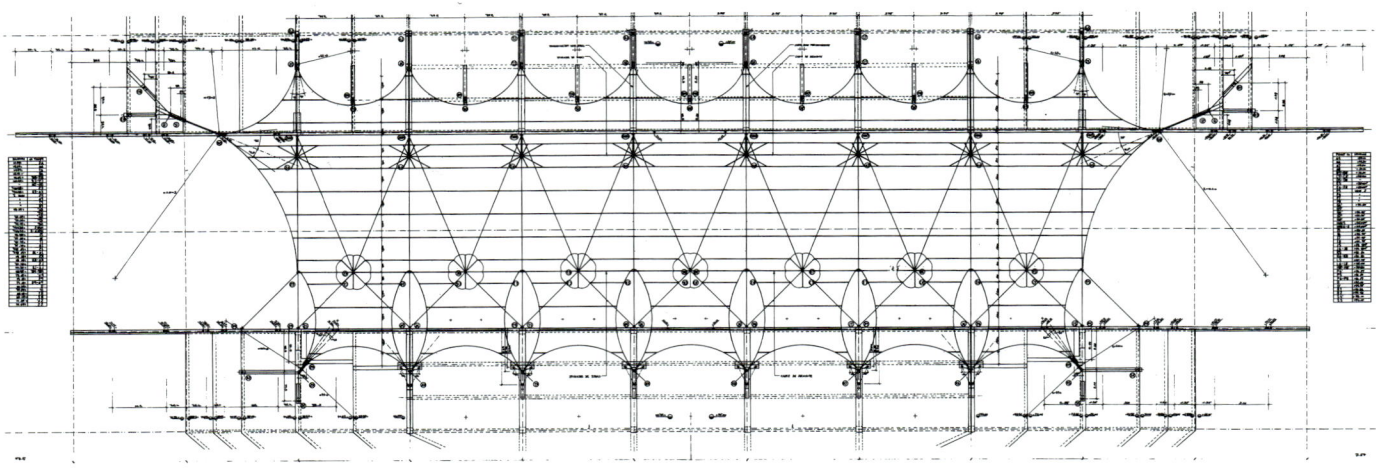

Schlumberger Factories | Renzo Piano

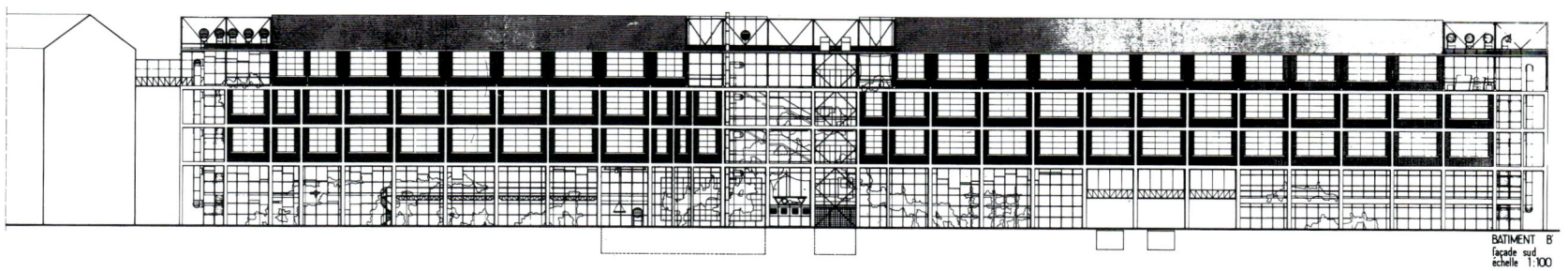

BATIMENT B'
façade sud
échelle 1:100

Lloyd's of London | London, England | 1981-1986

Richard Rogers

Lloyd's is located in the heart of the city of London's financial district. It is set in the tight fabric and medieval street pattern of the city.

As one approaches along the narrow city streets, views of the building gradually unfold the free-standing structural framework, translucent walls, terraces and glazed roof. In the process of reasserting the close-woven fabric of the historical city, the urban context was a key form generator. Lloyd's is built up out of repetitive and relatively autonomous detail, as well as out of honestly expressed materials and construction.

The main building is a simple rectangle. Six towers around the rectangle were created to contain lifts, toilets, kitchens, fire stairs and lobbies. Concentrating these elements into the satellite towers and supporting the main building on external columns gives an uninterrupted space within the enclosing envelope and minimises restrictions on use.

The most important single aspect of the design is *flexibility*. Lloyd's have already had to relocate twice this century, because of lack of space and the inability to adapt to changing circumstances. The building offers a system by which the elevations may be changed in response to needs within a controlled framework. The service equipment, mechanical services, lifts, toilets, kitchens, fire stairs and lobbies are easily accessible for maintenance and replaceable in case of obsolescence.

The building is designed as a series of concentric galleries overlooking a *central atrium*. In this way the several galleries were interlinked so that underwriters and brokers could see each other and so that business as a whole could flow smoothly. The central rectangular atrium rises the entire height of the building. This space illuminates the centres of the deep floors from above. Each gallery is used either as a part of the Underwriting Room or as optimum office space. All vertical movement within the Underwriting Room is by a central escalator system at the southern end of the atrium.

In spite of the complexity of the interior, the overall conception is supremely simple and logical. The service rooms are situated on the lower ground level. This is a semi-public area which houses the Lloyd's restaurant and coffee areas, wine bar, shops, library, meeting rooms and reception area. It is followed by the Room and its associated galleries, then the office space and finally the Chairman's Committee Rooms.

1933 Born in Florence, Italy.
1953-1959 Studied at the Architectural Association, London, England.
1961-1962 Studied at the School of Architecture, Yale University, New Haven, U.S.A.
1963-1967 Partnership with Norman and Wendy Foster and Su Rogers in Team 4.
1964, 1965, 1968 Architectural Design Award.
1967 Financial Times Industrial Architecture Award.
1968 Ideal Home House for Today Award.
1968-1970 Partnership with Su Rogers.
1971-1977 Partnership with Atelier Piano & Rogers.
1971 British Steel Corporation Design Award.
1976 Financial Times Industrial Architecture Award.
Since 1977 Partnership Richard Rogers and Partners.
1978 Auguste Perret Prize.
1982 Award for the Most Exceptional Steel Structure in France.
1983 Financial Times Industrial Architecture Award.
1984 Chair, School of Architecture, Yale University, New Haven, U.S.A.
1985 R.I.B.A. Gold Medal for Architecture.
1986 Chevalier de la Légion d'Honneur.
1987 Financial Times Industrial Architecture Award.
1988 Eternit International Prize for Architecture.
1989 R.I.B.A. Regional Award.

Member of the Royal Academy, London, England.
Honorary Fellow of the American Institute of Architects (A.I.A.).

Major works
1977 Georges Pompidou Centre, Paris, France (with Renzo Piano and Ove Arup).
1981-1986 Lloyd's of London, England.
1983 Industrial units and housing at Thames Wharf, London, England.

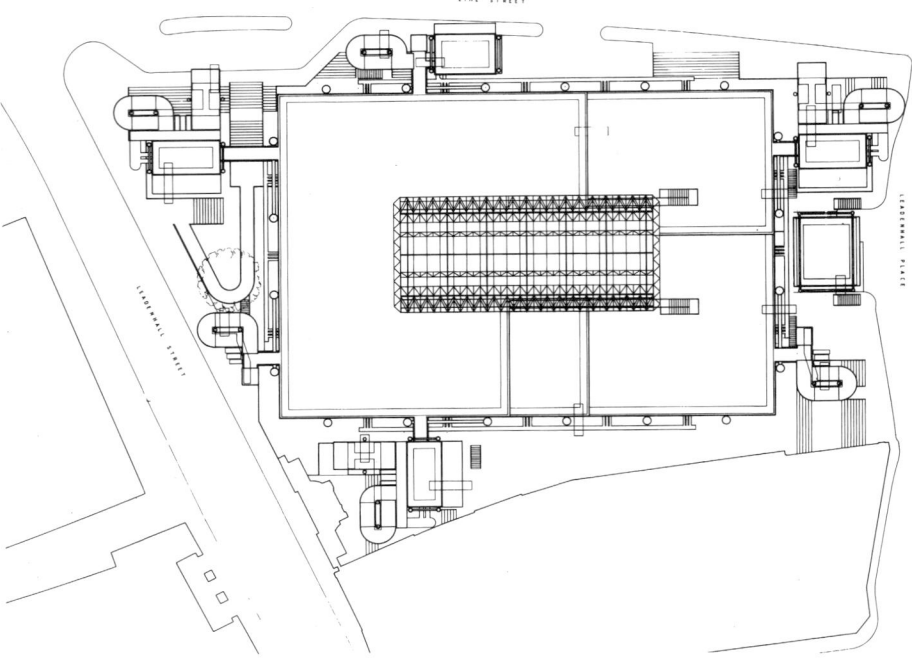

The building is twelve storeys to the north and steps down to six storeys towards the south, creating a series of terraces at various levels. The six towers define the street boundaries. The principal entrance of Leadenhall Street and Lime Street acts as a pivot to the whole scheme. Twelve external glazed lifts provide magnificent views across London.

The external glazing system is designed to modify dynamically the internal environment so that the air conditioning and lighting systems are highly effective in providing a visually comfortable quality of light and a substantial reduction in energy consumption. The structure of the building was conceived in concrete for its visual qualities and fire resistance. The six satellite towers consist of a precast concrete frame of columns and beams on which precast slabs are attached. Four of the six towers carry major plant rooms located above roof level. The service towers are clad in stainless steel sandwich panels with a one-hour fire rating. An outstanding feature of Lloyd's is the way the technical functions are expressed and used in the architecture.

Lloyd's of London | Richard Rogers

Friedrichstadt Housing Block | Berlin, West Germany | 1985-1987

Aldo Rossi

Before the Second World War Friedrichstadt was part of the centre of Berlin, but it was almost totally destroyed in 1945. The southern part of Friedrichstadt is now in West Berlin, at the edge of the city and close to the Wall. In the sixties and seventies several attempts were made to rebuild this part of the city, but the results were not very satisfactory. As part of the *'Internationale Bauausstellung Berlin 1984-87'*, the Bauausstellung Berlin Gmbh was given the task of drawing up plans in cooperation with architects for the redevelopment of Friedrichstadt. The first aim was to achieve a balance of housing, jobs and cultural and leisure activities. At the same time Friedrichstadt and the adjacent Kreuzberg district, which had a completely different structure, were to be brought into line with each other as far as possible. For Friedrichstadt a type of urban housing had to be developed which would cater for a very diverse local population. It was decided to commission several architects and to divide this sizeable district (six hectares) into a number of project areas for which competitions were organised. The competition for the design of the so-called Block 10, between Wilhelmstrasse, Kochstrasse, Friedrichstrasse and Puttkamerstrasse, was won by **Aldo Rossi** in 1980-81.

Rossi's aim was to respect the building lines of the streets and to place the buildings along the edges of the site. This would underline the limits of the block. This approach also fitted in best with the surviving buildings and with what had stood on the spot before 1945. **Rossi** included the surviving buildings in his design, so that the new block consists of both old and new structures. He wanted the new buildings to refer to the character of Berlin and of Friedrichstadt in particular.

Over the years, as a result of consultations with local residents, **Rossi's** plans underwent quite a few changes. In 1987 part of the project, at the corner of Kochstrasse and Wilhelmstrasse, was realised. This corner, the site of a huge column, is the most striking point in the block. The facades on the two streets are rather different from each other. The one on Kochstrasse is fairly closed in character. The entire facade is executed in brick and interrupted only by several staircases which are set back and topped by steep roofs. On the ground floor there is a kind of arcade or gallery with space for several shops. The facade on Wilhelmstrasse consists of brick surfaces alternating

1931 Born in Milan, Italy.
1955-1964 Editor of Casabella-Continuita.
1959 Graduated from the School of Architecture, Milan Polytechnic, Italy.
1959 Started an architectural office in Milan, Italy.
1965 Professor, School of Architecture, Milan Polytechnic, Italy.
1972-1975 Professor of Planning, Federal Polytechnic, Zürich, Switzerland.
1975 Professor of Architectural Composition, University of Venice, Italy.
1976 Professor, Cornell University, Ithaca, New York, U.S.A.
1976 Visiting Professor, Cooper Union School of Architecture, New York, U.S.A.
1980 Professor of Planning, Yale University, New Haven, U.S.A.
1983 Visiting Professor, Harvard Graduate School of Design, Cambridge, U.S.A.

Member of the Academy of San Luca, Rome, Italy.
Honorary member of the Association of German Architects (B.D.A.).
Honorary member of the American Institute of Architects (A.I.A.).

Major works
1970 Gallaratese apartment building, Milan, Italy.
1979-1981 Teatro del Mondo, Venice, Italy.
1985-1987 Friedrichstadt housing block, Berlin, West Germany.

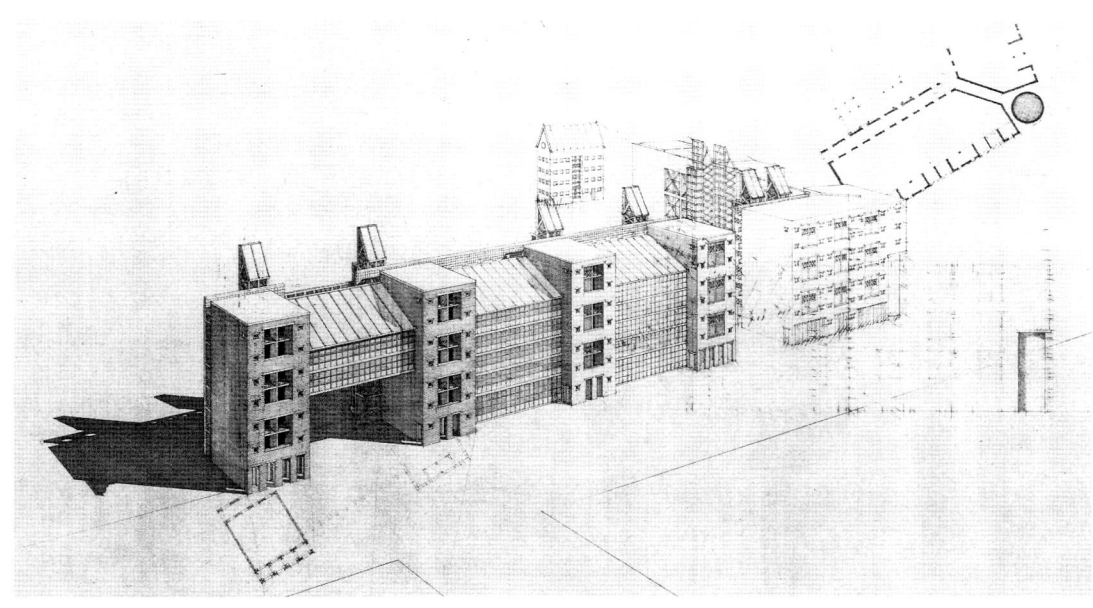

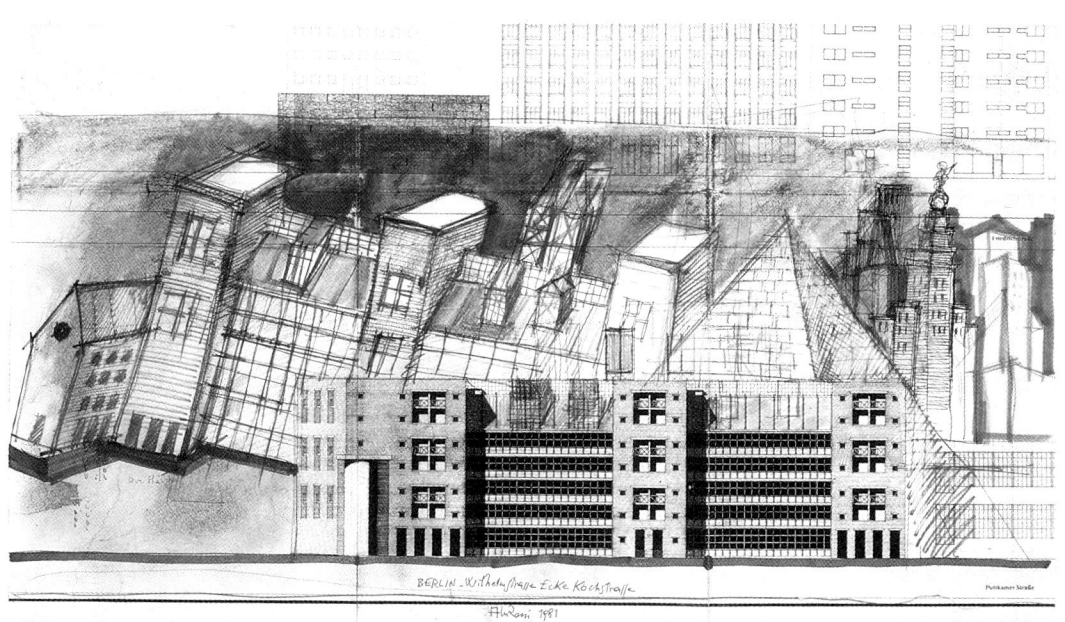

BERLIN - Wilhelmstraße Ecke Kochstraße

AlRossi 1981

with glass and steel curtain walls, so that it looks less closed than the one on Kochstrasse. The walls at the rear of the complex are plastered and broken by staircases in glass and brick.

Rossi used plain materials and simple techniques in this project in a deliberate attempt to harmonise as closely as possible with building practice in Berlin.

Friedrichstadt Housing Block | Aldo Rossi

Matosinhos is a medium-sized town not far from the provincial capital Oporto. Apart from a new city hall, there was a need for a range of cultural facilities including a library, a museum, a conservatory, studios for artists, ballet rooms, an exhibition hall, two auditoria and a municipal theatre. An extensive site was available and although there were some buildings on it they could be demolished. Several dwellings on the edge of the site were also ready to be pulled down. The fact that many facilities were to be brought together at one point in the town meant that a wide-ranging study of the planning aspects was necessary. In 1979 an architectural competition was organised. The proposals submitted had to include a design for the new city hall but also plans clearly indicating how the other facilities were to be incorporated in the future. There were 26 entries and **Alcino Soutinho** was the winner.

Soutinho's entry was an attempt to *reorganise the site by adding new elements to the existing buildings.* He wanted to integrate a nineteenth-century house at the centre of the site in the new architecture and turn it into a museum, without giving it undue emphasis. The house was to become a natural element in the overall concept. His plans were based on having several separate buildings, typologically clearly defined, distributed over the site. Streets, squares and greenery ensure that there is no sense of one great mass of buildings. The open spaces were related to the interiors of the public buildings.

Soutinho's project was intended as a long-term urban development plan. It was to be carried out in phases, so that it would be possible to involve other architects if required. The city hall was to have priority, but because of economic and political circumstances it was not completed until 1987, eight years after entries were invited for the competition.

The city hall is divided into several volumes, so that it does not lose touch with the proportions of the existing buildings on the site, and this is particularly evident from the rear. Despite this use of several volumes, typological unity in both interior and exterior has been preserved. The front consists of one long smooth facade with an arcade. It bulges slightly at the centre to emphasise the entrance. The exterior is completely covered in ochre veined marble. Inside, marble is also used together with other traditional materials

1930 Born in Vila Nova de Gaia, Portugal.
1957 Graduated from the School of Architecture, University of Oporto, Portugal.
1954-1964 Collaboration with Januario Godinho, José Carlos Loureiro, Amrénio Losa and Octavio Filqueiras.
1957 Started an architectural office.
1973 Professor, School of Architecture, University of Oporto, Portugal.
1984 AICA-SEC Prize for the Museum and City Hall at Amarante, Portugal.
1984 'Europa Nostra' International Prize for the Pousada de Vila Nova de Cerveira, Portugal.

Major works
1983 City Hall and Museum, Amarante, Portugal.
1984 Pousada de Vila Nova de Cerveira, Portugal.
1983-1987 City Hall, Matosinhos, Portugal.

Alcino Soutinho

City Hall | Matosinhos, Portugal | 1983-1987

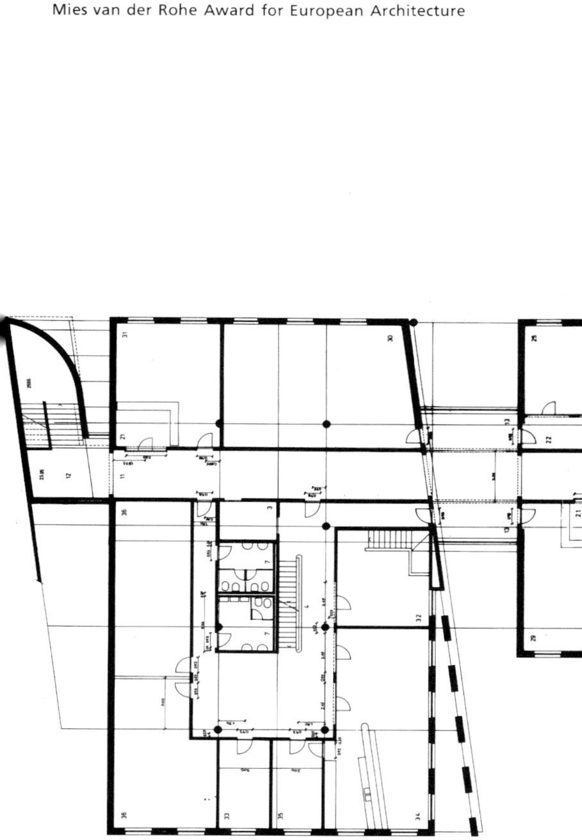

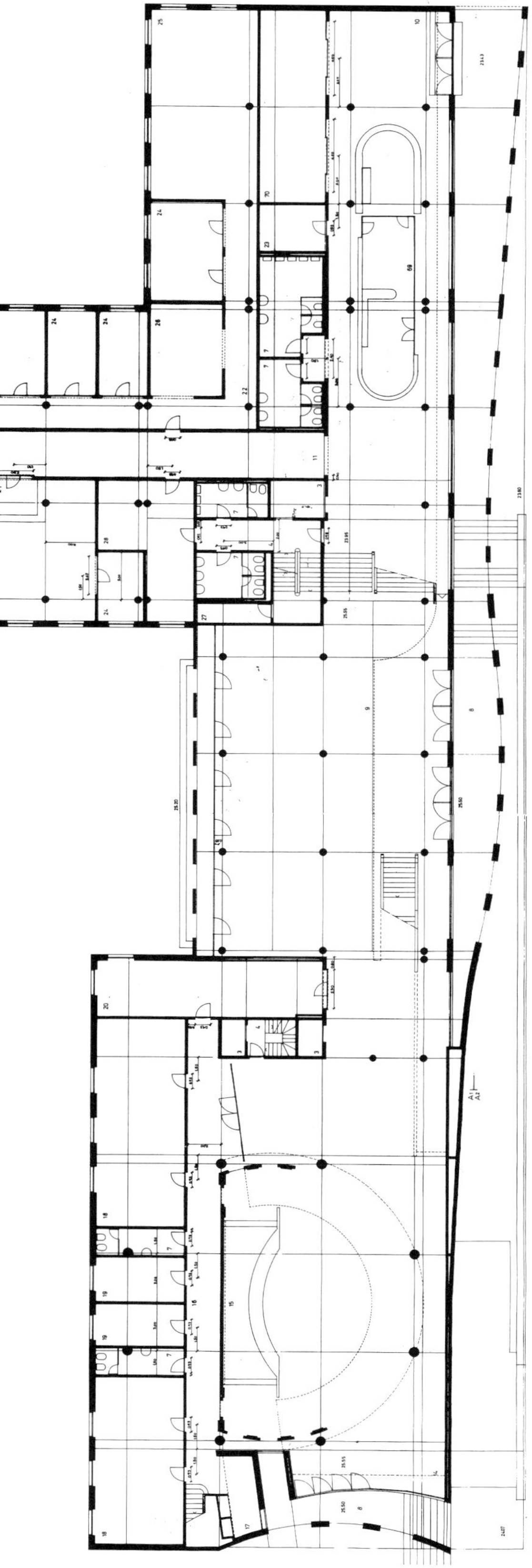

such as wood, tiles and stucco.

At the entrance there is an atrium rising through all five floors of the building. The other parts of the city hall can be reached from here. To the left there are two large council chambers one above the other and the offices of the mayor and aldermen. This part of the building has a domed roof. To the right are the areas for the public services departments. Galleries on each floor lead to the part housing the administration, secretariat and maintenance department. On some floors the centre of this gallery is reserved for the public and the two sides for staff. The centre is divided off by glass walls.

Outside, at the rear of the building, there is a small square which is more or less enclosed by the city hall and the nineteenth-century house. This square is related to the entrance and can be regarded as a visual extension of it.

City Hall | Alcino Soutinho

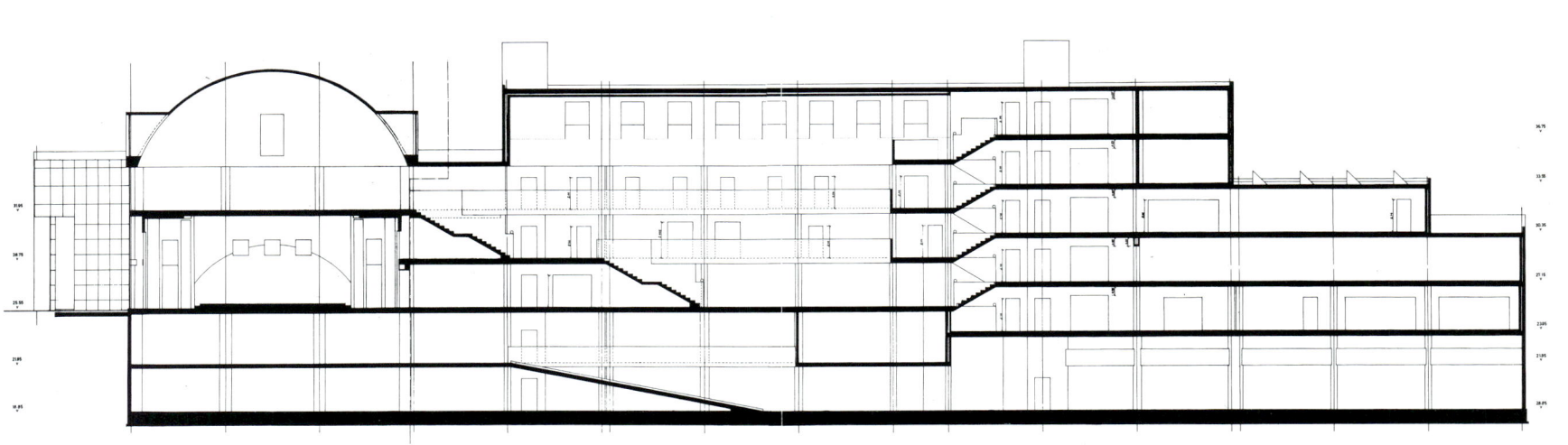

Clore Gallery | London, England | 1982-1987

In 1980 the Clore foundation commissioned **James Stirling** and **Michael Wilford** Associates to build an extension for the Tate Gallery in London to house the **Turner** collection.

This new wing which Stirling designed has two arms, one of which connects to the old building constructed in 1897. The other, attached at right angles, aligns with a nineteenth-century porter's lodge of a former hospital. The nine exhibition rooms where **Turner's** work is exhibited are on the first floor of the long arm of the L-shaped extension. Two of these rooms have been designed for the paintings from the depot collection, which will be regularly on view to the public. The new rooms, which vary in size and shape, are directly accessible from the exhibition rooms in the old building and are on the same level. Coming from the Tate Gallery, the visitor enters the new wing at the first exhibition room on the first floor. At right angles to this **Stirling** has placed a slightly narrower room of equal length, flanked on its two long sides by two smaller rooms. One of the smaller east rooms has a bay overlooking the garden and the River Thames. Natural light is used to illuminate the exhibition rooms by means of roof lanterns. Curved ceiling panels reflect the light onto the exhibition walls. A combination of daylight and artificial light is also possible and the daylight can even be shut out of the rooms altogether.

The ground floor accommodates the educational space, an auditorium seating 180, a space for paper conservation, the administrative offices, a study, a reading room overlooking the garden and an entrance hall.

Apart from the most popular entrance via the Tate Gallery, the Clore Gallery can also be reached from the ground floor via the garden and the terrace on the east side. The garden has two gravel paths leading to a paved terrace with a pond and pergola. On the north side of the terrace is the entrance to the Clore Gallery, which has deliberately not been oriented to the river to avoid competing with the main entrance to the Tate. There is also a third, smaller entrance at the rear of the new wing.

The terrace entrance to the Clore Gallery opens into a low hall, where the information desk is situated. This low hall takes on a monumental aspect when seen from the staircase leading up to the exhibition rooms. Above the staircase the space opens into a high, narrow, illuminated slit. The staircase

James Stirling

1926 Born in Glasgow, Scotland.

1942 Studied at the Liverpool School of Art, Liverpool, England.

1945-1950 Studied at the School of Architecture, University of Liverpool, England.

1950-1952 Studied at the School of Town Planning and Regional Research, London, England.

1953-1956 Worked as Senior Assistant at Lyons, Israel and Ellis, London, England.

1955 Visiting Lecturer, Architectural Association, London, England.

1956-1957 Visiting Lecturer, Polytechnic of Regent Street, England.

1956-1963 Partnership with James Gowan, London, England.

1964-1970 Started an architectural office in London, England.

1967 Visiting Professor, School of Architecture, Yale University, New Haven, U.S.A.

Since 1971 Partnership with Michael Wilford.

1976 Awarded the Brunner Award by the National Institute of Arts and Letters, U.S.A.

1977 Visiting Professor, Academy of Arts, Düsseldorf, West Germany.

1978 Alvar Aalto Medal, Finland.

1980 Royal Gold Medal for Architecture.

1981 Pritzker Prize.

Member of the Royal Institute of British Architects (R.I.B.A.).

Major works

1955-1958 Flats at Ham Common, London, England.

1959-1963 Engineering building, Leicester University, England.

1977-1984 New building and chamber theatre for the Neue Staatsgalerie, Stuttgart, West Germany.

1982-1987 Clore Gallery, London, England.

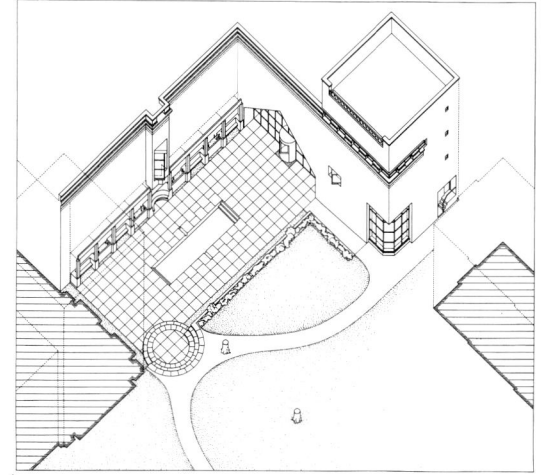

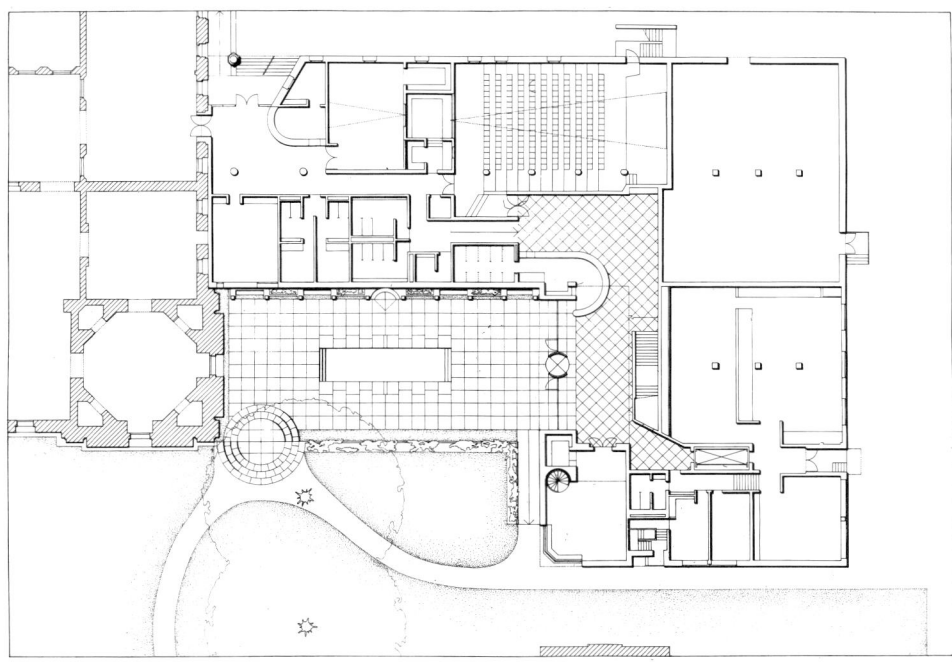

gives access to a long gallery from which the museum rooms can be reached. Colour plays an important role. Two basic colours, off-white and an orangey beige, are used throughout the Clore Gallery for spaces outside the exhibition rooms, in the lobby and auditorium, for instance. Colour accents have been added. The banisters of the staircase are pink, and the casing of the large, arched opening directing the visitor to the exhibition rooms is a turquoise-ultramarine colour. The walls of the rooms where **Turner's** works are displayed are a warm grey.

The exterior of the Clore Gallery links up with the adjoining buildings in use of materials and detail. The Ionic-Doric cornice of the Tate Gallery has been repeated in the new building, tying in with the eaves of the porter's lodge on the other side. The rusticated base of the Tate Gallery is picked up on the terrace side of the new building in a pergola of the same height. The most striking feature of the frontispieces, however, is the *grid of horizontal and vertical stone ribs filled with stucco or brick*. **Stirling** uses this to mark the transition from the Tate Gallery, for which Portland stone was mostly used, and the porter's lodge, which is built mainly of brick. The grid is repeated on the rear gable, where the new wing similarly adjoins the Tate building. The north-east and south-east elevations have no linking function and are constructed of light-coloured stone.

Clore Gallery | James Stirling

Gatehouse | Frankfurt am Main | 1983-1986

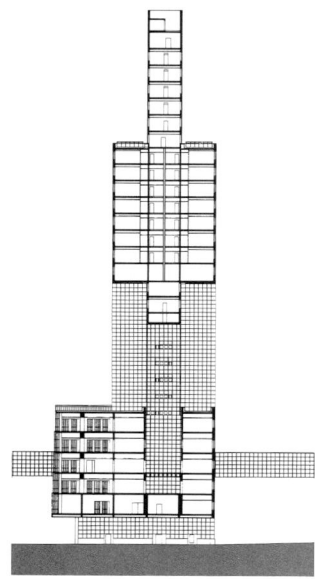

20

The Frankfurt Trade Fair is situated to the south of Theodor-Heuss-Allee in Frankfurt am Main. Railway lines traverse the fair grounds, creating an open triangular space where they overpass, and dividing the grounds into two separate sections known as the East and West Terrains. The lines are an obstacle to fair activity and **Ungers** set out to find a solution that would literally get round them. His main objective was to unite the two terrains with an attractive yet functional building.

From a spatial viewpoint, the *track triangle* occupies a crucial position. **Ungers** gave this visual emphasis by constructing a striking building with a symbolic and thematic function. A high-rise construction was seen as appropriate for the urban setting. The building conspicuously marks its central fair-ground location and the convergence of the two main traffic axes on the terrain.

The bridging plan for the track-triangle comprises two main components, the base construction and the high-rise emerging from it. The base occupies the entire space between the two railway lines. The general service operations for the fair are accommodated in this section. Shopping facilities, facilities for the press, general amenities, etc. are located here at five levels. The south-eastern corner of the building houses the heating system. This area is distinguished from the rest of the base construction by a *cut in the facade*, while remaining visually integrated into the building as a whole. Two passages for pedestrians will traverse the base construction and emerge as glass tubes on the outside of the building, bridging the railway lines on both sides of the base construction. The base construction is capped with an accessible platform at the height of 27 metres. Above this platform the main building rises another 24 floors. Altogether the entire construction has 29 storeys and rises to a full height of 115 metres.

The high-rise consists of two body types set one inside the other: an inner house of glass and an outer house of stone. The combined effect is one of a gigantic gate or an oversized window. *The gate stands as a symbol of the Frankfurt Fair as international trading centre, as well as visually linking the fair's segregated terrains.* Its position near the western highway exit for Frankfurt also means the high-rise acts as a gateway to the city. The stone house accommodates mainly offices. The upper, protruding glass section is

Oswald Mathias Ungers

1926 Born in Kaisersesch, West Germany.
1947-1950 Studied Architecture at the Technical University of Karlsruhe, West Germany.
1950 Started an architectural office in Cologne, West Germany.
1963 Professor, Technical University of Berlin, West Germany.
1964 Started an architectural office in Berlin, West Germany.
1965, 1967 Visiting Critic, Cornell University, Ithaca, New York, U.S.A.
1965-1967 Dean of the Faculty of Architecture and Senator of the Technical University of Berlin, West Germany.
1969-1975 Chairman of the Department of Architecture, Cornell University, Ithaca, New York, U.S.A.
1970 Started an architectural office in Ithaca, U.S.A.
1973 Professor at Harvard University, U.S.A.
1974-1975 Professor of Architecture, University of California, Los Angeles, U.S.A.
1975 Full Professor of Architecture, Cornell University, Ithaca, New York, U.S.A.
1976 Started an architectural office in Frankfurt am Main, West Germany.
1978 Professor, Harvard University, U.S.A.
1979-1980 Professor, Academy for Applied Arts, Vienna, Austria.
1983 Started an architectural office in Karlsruhe, West Germany.
1986 Professor of Architecture, Academy of Arts, Düsseldorf, West Germany.
1987 Prize of the Association of German Architects (B.D.A.).
1989 Rhénan Prize, Strasbourg, France.

Member of the Academy of San Luca, Rome, Italy.
Member of the American Institute of Architects (A.I.A.).
Member of the Association of German Architects (B.D.A.).
Member of the Academy of Sciences of Berlin, West Germany.

Major works
1979-1984 Museum of Architecture, Frankfurt am Main, West Germany.
1980-1983 Hall No. 9 at the Trade Fair, Frankfurt am Main, West Germany.
1983-1986 Gatehouse at the Trade Fair, Frankfurt am Main, West Germany.

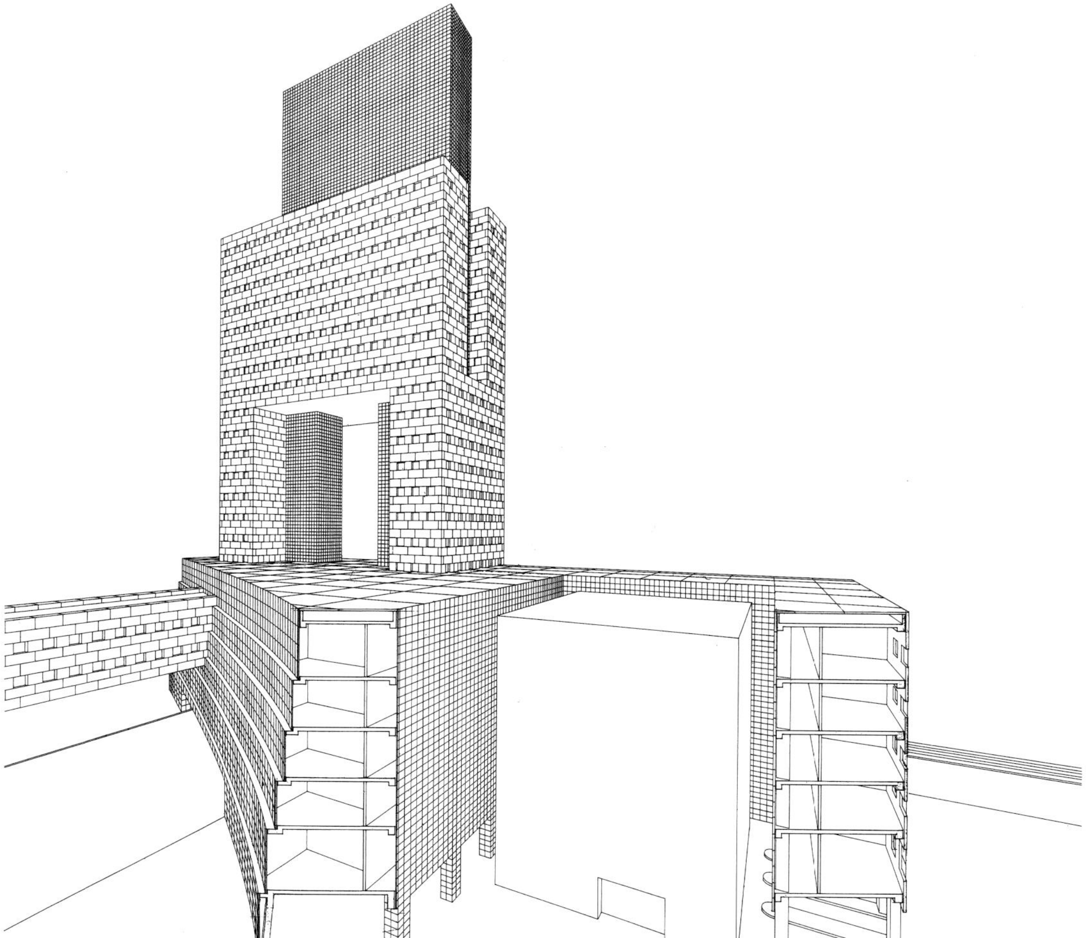

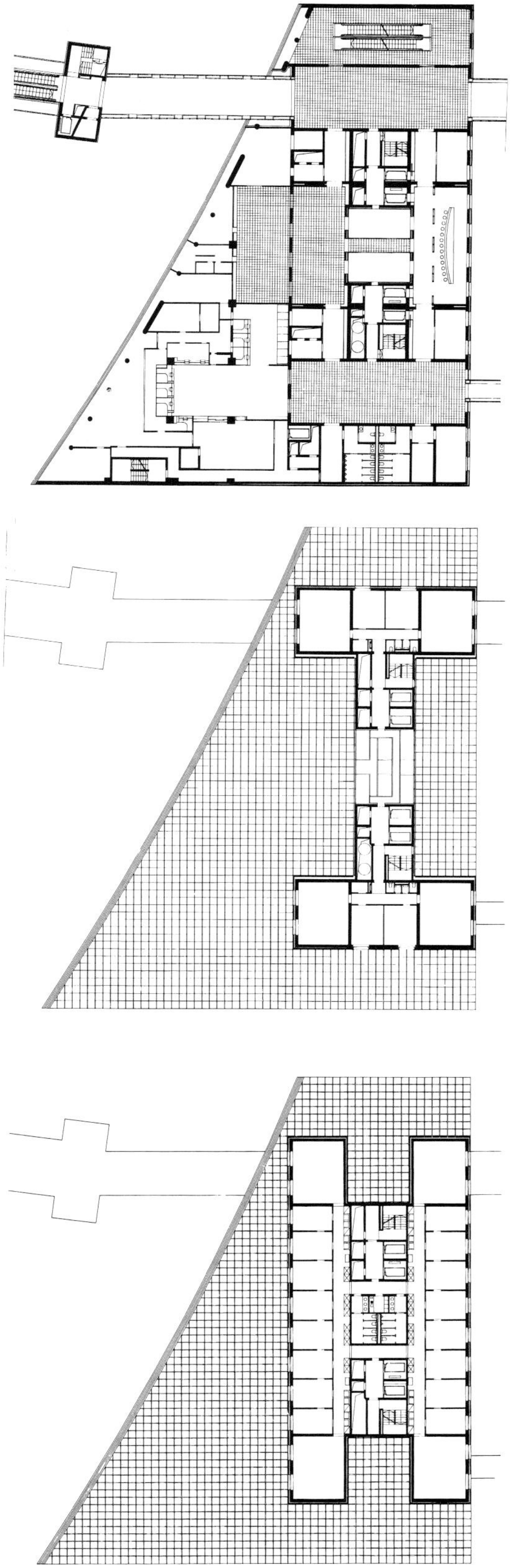

the real representative area, combining the panoramic conference rooms of the top floors with the spacious void of the lower floors.

Ungers uses grids of glazing for the *window* aspects of the scheme. The facade of the building comprises a glass curtain of green mirror glass and red sandstone plates. Both glass and sandstone plates were subsequently used to enclose the concrete core.

The main object of the plan was not so much to concentrate a large construction on a relatively small plot, but to transcend the functional requirements of this type of building, the high-rise, and create a new variation and give it a distinctive identity.

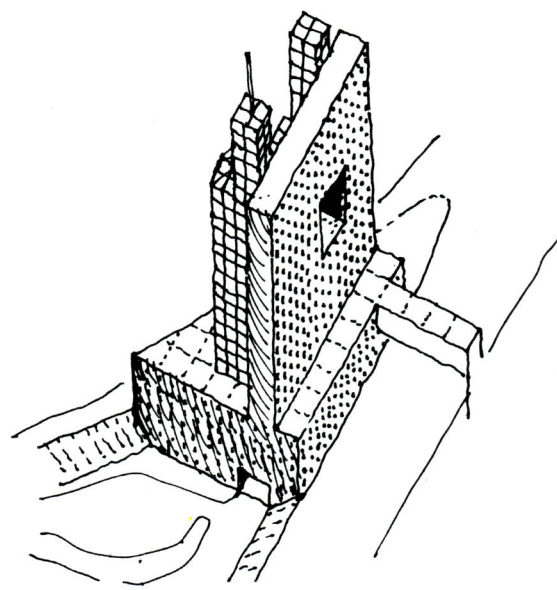

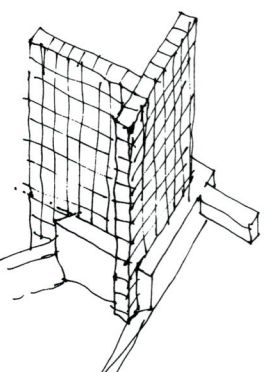

Gatehouse | Oswald Mathias Ungers

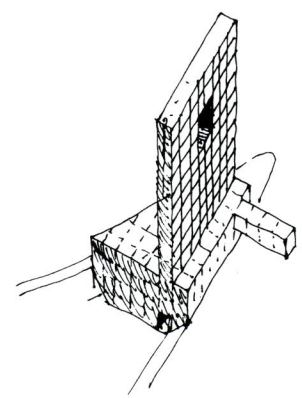

Housing on Giudecca | Venice, Italy | 1980-1986

Gino Valle

In 1980 **Gino Valle** was commissioned to design a complex of 94 dwellings on the island of Giudecca in Venice. The rectangular site lay in an industrial area bounded by canals on the east and west sides. There was a large garden on the north side and behind it an old cement factory in neo-Gothic style known as the *Mulino Stucky*. The garden covered the entire width of the building site. A canal was to be built on the south side of the site to mark the border between the new housing and the southern part of the island, where there were factories and beyond them a large lagoon.

Valle's design for the project showed the greatest respect for the existing environment. One of his chief concerns was to retain the Via dei Lavranieri, a street running straight across the island from east to west, and the garden in front of the cement factory. He designed a housing block of a closed character in a style which accorded with that of the factory buildings in the immediate surroundings. The pattern of transverse rows of housing on an east-west axis is also a reference to the existing buildings on the island. Moreover, the complex is in brick, like the *Mulino Stucky*.

The central part consists of a number of parallel housing blocks which decrease in height, from four to two storeys, from north to south. On the east and west sides there is a line of five *towers* four storeys high. They provide a visual delineation of the limits of the site.

The buildings had to meet several requirements. The maximum height was to be four storeys, and they had to be designed so that the living room of an apartment had a view of the lagoon. Each dwelling was to have its own entrance, and so **Valle** did not use common staircases. Standard sizes for the rooms in the new houses had been fixed, and **Valle** worked on the basis of a *module* of 165 × 165 centimetres. This was derived from the brick material used for the project. The use of this module produced apartments of three different surface areas: 46, 70 and 90 square metres. They have C-shaped ground plans and are positioned around a small courtyard.

The first block, on the north side, contains seventeen apartments of 90 square metres and four of 70 square metres. Access is via a gallery on the first floor. The kitchen and living room are on the upper floor, from where there are good views of both the old part of Venice to the north and the lagoon to the south. The balcony faces south. The second row of housing

1923 Born in Udine, Italy.
1948 Graduated from the School of Architecture, Venice, Italy.
1951 Received a Fulbright Scholarship to study at the Harvard Graduate School of Design, Cambridge, U.S.A.
1952 Started an architectural office.
1952 Bachelor's degree in City and Regional Planning.
1952 Professor, C.I.A.M. International School, Venice, Italy.
1956, 1962, 1963 Golden Compass.
1962-1963 Course coordinator and Professor of Industrial Design, Venice, Italy.
1965 Annual Lectureship of the Royal Institute of British Architects (R.I.B.A.).
1967-1971 Taught in U.S.A., Europe and South Africa.
1967-1971 Vice-President of the International Council of Societies of Industrial Design (I.C.S.I.D.), Brussels, Belgium.
1977 Professor, School of Architecture, Venice, Italy.
1983-1985 Member of the Design Advisory Committee, Salzburg, Austria.
1988 Antonio Feltrinelli Prize.

Member of the Academy of San Luca, Rome, Italy.

Major works
1980-1983 I.B.M. Centre, Basiano, Milan, Italy.
1980-1986 Housing on Giudecca, Venice, Italy.
1981-1983 Banca Commerciale Italiana, New York, U.S.A.
1984-1986 I.B.M. Europe office, Paris, France.

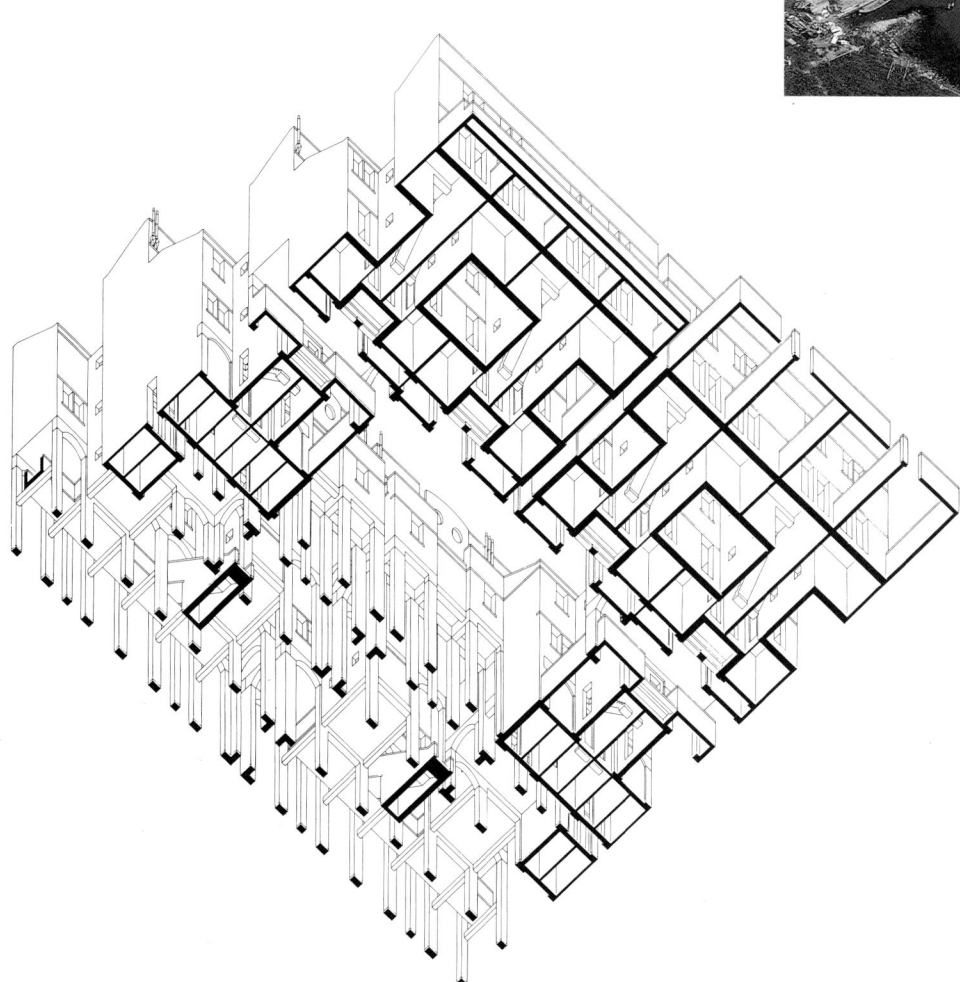

consists of sixteen maisonettes of 70 square metres. The entrance is on the ground floor and the living room is on the upper floor, with a view to the south. The third row consists of twenty maisonettes of 70 square metres with bedrooms on the first floor and the living room on the ground floor facing south. The last block beside the southern canal contains the smaller apartments of 46 square metres.

The closed character of the lower floors of the apartments contrasts sharply with the open character of the upper floors. The fall of light plays an important part here. The lower floors are rather dark, but as one goes up the light increases. The fall of light has clearly been taken into account in the arrangement of the balconies and the height of the ceilings.

The *towers* along the eastern and western canals have apartments of 46 square metres and maisonettes of 90 square metres. They are designed on the same lines as the rows of housing in the centre. Here too the floor plan of the apartments is C-shaped, but the courtyards are replaced by terraces. Between the towers there are narrow streets providing access to the canal, but from a distance they nonetheless appear to form a solid line. This optical illusion is created by the use of the motif of a broken tympanum, which arises from the slope of the roofs.

Within the rectangular complex **Valle** designed a network of paths, narrow streets and porticos which open up a small, central square, the *Campiello*. On the south side the row of housing along the canal does not continue right across, so that space is left for a so-called *Campazzo*.

Housing on Giudecca | Gino Valle

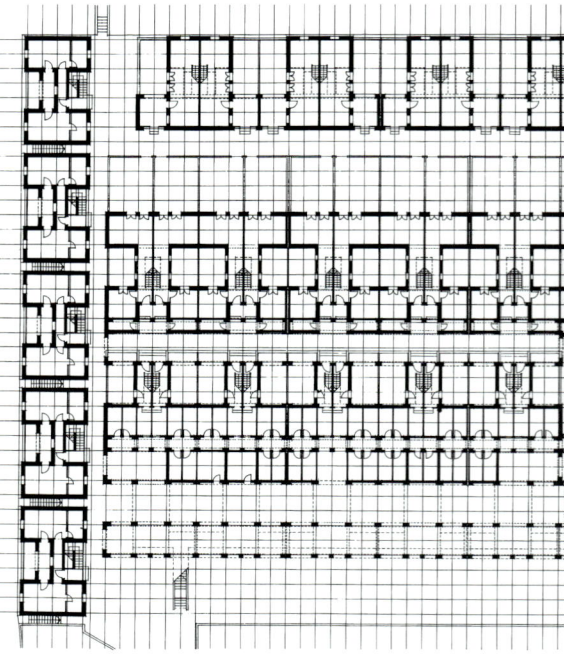

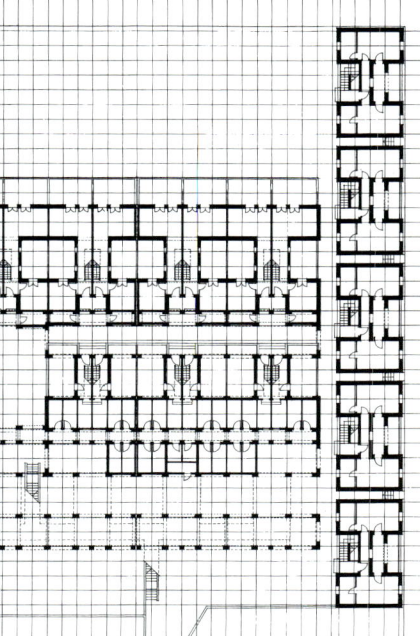

In 1969 a major earthquake in Sicily reduced the towns and villages in the Valle del Belice to not much more than rubble. Twelve years later, in 1981, the mayor of the newly constructed town of Gibellina Nuova, **Ludovico Corrao**, asked **Francesco Venezia** to develop a plan for incorporating the remnants of an elegant neo-classicist facade into the architecture of Gibellina Nuova. The facade of the Palazzo Di Lorenzo was the only surviving fragment of the old, completely abandoned town of Gibellina. Thus the problem consisted of dismantling the old facade, transporting it to a new location a good 20 kilometres away, and reassembling it.

To **Venezia**, Gibellina Nuova appeared so desolate that it almost acquired a character of its own. The new town bore almost no relation at all to the surrounding landscape with its hills and mountains in which the old settlement was once embedded and to which its ruins now returned.

It was decided to reassemble the facade in a hidden, self-contained location within the new settlement and to integrate it into an architectural complex of similar dimensions enclosing a courtyard. In this way a conflict with the new buildings of the town which would have dwarfed the facade with their sheer size was avoided.

Venezia wanted the new building in which the old fragment was to be incorporated to present a harmonious whole. At the same time *the character of the facade should be preserved so that it would still be recognizable as a ruin even in its new location.* **Venezia** felt it was important to reconstruct the old facade in relation to the surrounding landscape and to locate the new building at the edge of the town, close to the campagna, with a long approach path through a terraced garden. Great attention was given to the few characteristic aspects of the new location, such as the monotony of the new settlement, the sloping terrain and the simple structure of the farmhouse on the neighbouring hill.

The interior in which the fragment of the facade of the Palazzo Di Lorenzo stands is a patio surrounded on three sides by walls and on the fourth by a narrow building. The ambiguous relationship between interior and exterior is one of the central themes of the building. Shadow plays an important role. The moving line of sunlight interacting with the fixed elements in various ways creates a constantly changing play of shadows and indicates the

1944 Born in Lauro, Italy.
1970 Graduated from the School of Architecture, Naples, Italy.
1970 Started an architectural office.
1971 Teacher, School of Architecture, Naples, Italy.
1986 Chair, School of Architecture, Naples, Italy.
1987 Visiting Professor, Sommerakademie in Berlin, West Germany.
1988 Visiting Professor, Graduate School of Design, Harvard University, Cambridge, U.S.A.
1988 Professor in Architectural Design, School of Architecture, Genoa, Italy.
1988 European Community Architectural Prize.
1989 Visiting Professor, Federal Polytechnic, Lausanne, Switzerland.

Major works
1973-1976 Square in Lauro, Italy.
1981-1987 Museum in Gibellina, Italy.
1983-1986 Open-air Theatre, Salemi, Italy.

Francesco Venezia

Museum | Gibellina, Italy | 1981-1987

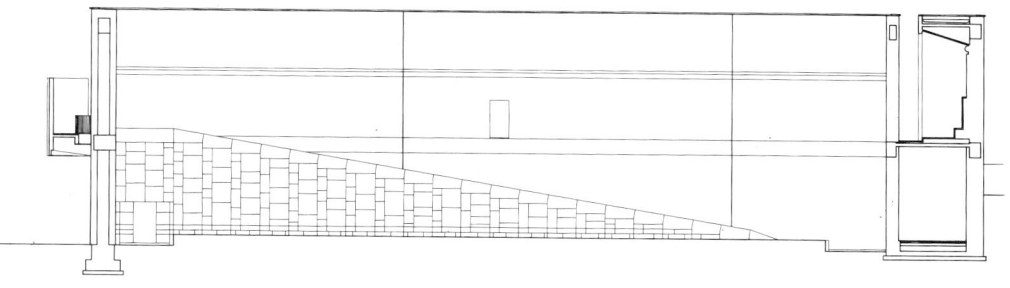

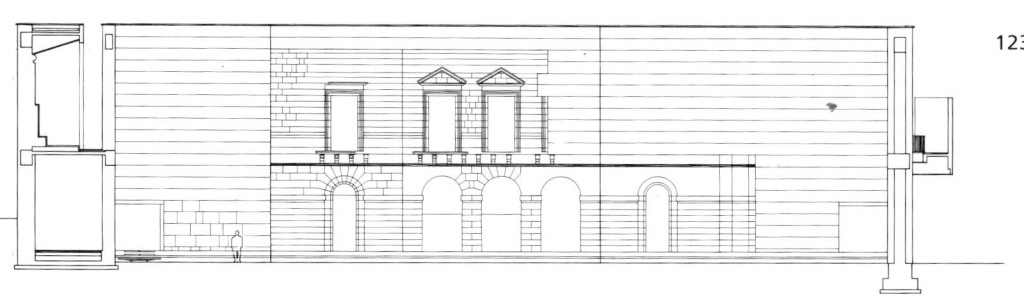

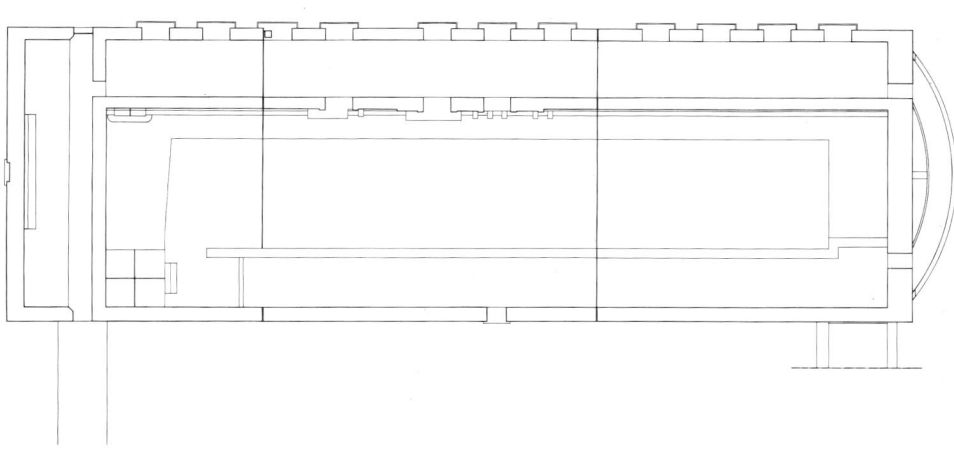

passage of time.

Access to the patio is via an inset, walled path bordering a garden planned as a continuation of the hillside. The facade is mounted on the inner side of the building. On the lower level there is a long room displaying a graphic arts collection and on the upper level there is a gallery opening on to both the interior and the countryside. On the south side of the patio a suspended passageway links a balustraded ramp with the gallery on the second floor. On the opposite side a restful atmosphere, a *riposo* is created by the cool shade resulting from the idea of enlarging and extending the north wall. Between the freshly cut stone slabs and the irregularly chipped edges of the old facade fragment runs a clearly visible joint four centimetres wide. A second joint subdivides the facade into two different areas and restores some of the lost symmetry. Both joints are echoed in the pavement of the court, ending at the opposite wall with its single aperture.

Three quarries were used for the stone. The stone dressing of the slabs was carried out on site to ensure continuity between the blocks of any one course and to give more emphasis to horizontal than to vertical joints. The building of stone walls required a high level of skill. Techniques that were abandoned along with the old town were rediscovered and the skill of the master masons revealed.

Museum | Francesco Venezia

Institutional and official credits

Committee of Honour
Enrique Baron, President of the European Parliament
Jean Dondelinger, Member of the Commission in Charge of
Cultural Affairs
Carlo Ripa di Meana, Member of the Commission in Charge of
the Environment, Nuclear Security and Civil Protection
Pasqual Maragall, Mayor of Barcelona
Xavier Rubert de Ventós, Member of the European Parliament

Jury Members
Kenneth Frampton, U.K., President of the Jury
Hans Hollein, Vienna
Vittorio Gregotti, Milan
François Burckhardt, Paris
Ricardo Bofill, Barcelona
Ignasi de Solà-Morales, Barcelona, Secretary of the Jury
Alessandro Giulianelli, Former Personal Representative of the
E.E.C. Cultural Commissioner

Committee of Experts
Jacques Lucan, France
Jean Louis Cohen, France
Wilfred Wang, United Kingdom
Peter Buchanan, United Kingdom
Francesco Dal Co, Italy
Claudia Conforti, Italy
Geert Bekaert, Belgium
Manuel Mendes, Portugal
Anton Gonzalez Capitel, Spain
Josep Lluís Mateo, Spain
Wolfgang Pehnt, West Germany
Ulrike Jehle, West Germany
Orestes B. Dumanis, Greece
Aristides Romanos, Greece
Hans van Dijk, The Netherlands
Shane de Blacam, Ireland
Hans Aspoeck, Denmark

**Representatives of the Mies van der Rohe Foundation
and the E.E.C.**
René André, Director in Charge of Cultural Action in the General Direction
of the Commission of Information, Communication and Culture
Lluís Hortet, Director of the Mies van der Rohe Foundation,
Barcelona

With special thanks to:
Meritxell Cuspinera
Eduard Maynés
Susana Landrove
Fabian Llonch
All the personnel in the candidates' offices who made the project materials
available

Aulenti, Gae
Mimmo Jodice
Deidi von Schaewen

Bosch, Theo
Jan Derwig
Flip Fahrenfort

Botta, Mario
Paola Palazetti
Pino Musi

Calatrava, Santiago
Eugeni Bofill / FRIS
Lluís Casals

Ciriani, Henri
Marcela Ciriani
Deidi von Schaewen
Stéphane Couturier
J.M. Monthiers

Colquhoun / Miller
Robert H. Mattheus
(portrait)
Peter Cook
Martin Charles

Foster, Norman
Andrew Ward (portrait)
Richard Davies

Gaudin, Henri
Deidi von Schaewen
Gaston Bergeret

Hertzberger, Herman
Ger van der Vlugt

Holzbauer, Wilhelm
Jeroen Nooter
Martha Deltsios

Martorell / Bohigas / Mackay
Lluís Casals

Moneo, Rafael
Lluís Casals

Natalini, Adolfo
Mario Ciampi

Nouvel, Jean
Deidi von Schaewen
Arnaud Bauman
(portrait)

Peichl, Gustav
Uwe Rau

Piano, Renzo
Deidi von Schaewen

Rogers, Richard
Richard Bryant / ARCAID
Peter Wedgewood
(portrait)

Rossi, Aldo
Uwe Rau

Siza, Alvaro
Eugeni Bofill / FRIS

Soutinho, Alcino
Luís Ferreira Alves

Stirling, James
Richard Bryant / ARCAID

Ungers, Oswald Mathias
Uwe Rau
Dieter Leistner

Valle, Gino
Dida Biggi
Paolo Giordano
(portrait)

Venezia, Francesco
By architect

Cover photographs
Eugeni Bofill / FRIS

Colophon

This publication is a co-operation between the
Mies van der Rohe Foundation and V+K Publishing

Project co-ordination
Diane Gray, Mies van der Rohe Foundation

Editing
Flos Wildschut
Thieu Knibbeler

Editorial direction
Stina van der Ploeg, V+K Publishing

Art direction
Cees W. de Jong, V+K Publishing

Design
Jan Johan ter Poorten, V+K Design

Translation
Karen Gamester
John Rudge

Printing/Typesetting
Snoeck-Ducaju & Zoon

The texts are based on articles and publications that have appeared over the years in connection with the projects and architects concerned.
We have also compiled a list of photographic credits.
By any omission, kindly contact either the Mies van der Rohe Foundation, Barcelona, or V+K Publishing, Laren.